CONCILIUM

Theology in the Age of Renewal

CONCILIUM

Theology in the Age of Renewal

Volume 54: Ecumenism

POST-ECUMENICAL CHRISTIANITY

Edited by

Hans Küng

Herder and Herder

1970
HERDER AND HERDER
232 Madison Avenue, New York 10016

CONTENTS $\frac{262}{P84k}$

5

PART II

DOCUMENTATION CONCILIUM

Hans Küng

Editorial

Post-Ecumenical Era?
Some Practical Considerations

IT IS a not particularly happy development that theology should be increasingly plagued with the ambiguous slogans or catch-phrases which characterize life today in general: phrases which have the power to rouse feelings, but which can simultaneously exclude thought and detract from action. The phrase "post-ecumenical era" belongs to this category, and in this issue we attempt to examine it as a positive challenge. The following two aspects are in urgent need of investigation:

1. There still exist extremely serious *differences*—both in theory and in practice—between the various Churches; these have un-fortunately not only been rendered outdated and obsolete by the development of the modern world, but have a more than nega-tive influence on the very position of the Churches in the secular world. For this reason it is essential that they should be thoroughly resolved.

2. The *mutual* problems of the Churches in the face of the secular world fortunately serve to balance inter-confessional dif-ferences to a large degree. It is precisely this confrontation of all the Churches with the secular world which stimulates desire to solve the doctrinal problems which separate them..

Various opinions are expressed in this issue. Their very diver-gence serves to emphasize the common ground they share. Here, too, theory is to be taken as an appeal for action.

PART I
ARTICLES

Yves Congar

Do the New Problems
of our Secular World
make Ecumenism Irrelevant?

I. Post-Ecumenism and Secular Ecumenism

THE late head of the W.C.C. information service, Philippe Maury, declared in 1966: "Many young people today are turning away from the ecumenical movement itself, and not just from its institutional manifestations—the ecumenical Council, youth movements, Christian organizations; they are demanding that the movement be widened to a generalized, simply human ecumenism, that does not take Christianity as a criterion."[1] At the same time, we read in *The Ecumenist*: "Post-ecumenism means primarily the development of a new understanding of the Church, a sense of standing at the heart of the Christian experience in history in all its variety; without abandoning our original tradition, we can understand it better if we see it in the context of a wider reality."[2] It seems to me that these two quotations are fairly representative. They express what is sometimes called post-ecumenism, whose special mark is a new awareness of the following things:

1. In our present understanding, being a Christian does not define one's position in the Church, but one's situation of being a believer in a world in a state of development. Aware of being a minority or diaspora, such Christians do not want to be limited

---

[1] "L'Eglise dans le monde", *Eglises en dialogue*, no. 2 (Tours, 1966), p. 89.
[2] Vol. 5 (Nov.–Dec. 1966); quoted by Charles Davis, *A Question of Conscience*. He refers also to G. Vahanian, in *Continuum* (1966), pp. 50–62.

by the framework of their own churches: they take the fact of
being Christians to involve a commitment to serve the world and
a responsibility to others. Though we may say that all this means
is that they are conscious of having a mission, that mission is
seen to flow simply from the fact of being a Christian, not from
concern with any kind of mandate of mission *from* some legally
established body. On the other hand, their will to unite with
other Christians goes without saying. If this is what ecumenism
is, then it must be said that ecumenism is a normal and spontaneous attitude for the people of God. This was very clear, for
instance, at the third World Congress of the Lay Apostolate,
held in Rome in October 1967.

2. Christians are very much aware of the problems of justice
and development, of poverty and the will to revolution all over
the world. The mass media bring everyone together. The Chinese
cultural revolution, Cuba, Ché Guevara, Latin America, the
students' revolts, American Black Power, the terrifyingly evident
needs of the Third World, Vietnam: all these have, in a very
short time, created an economic and political consciousness
which tends to lead on to a pre-revolutionary state of mind. The
Conference on "Church and Society" in Geneva in July 1966
was typical: the sense of the tragic divisions among men—blacks
and whites, the rich and the poor, the starving and the over-
fed—far outweighed any sense of the divisions among Christians.[3]

3. The questions being asked of theology and the Churches
are primarily questions from the world. It is the world which
directs the programme and puts the questions, questions concerning not only the world, but the Church. "The fundamental
ecumenical dialogue is therefore not the inter-Church dialogue
among different Christian sects, but the dialogue in which Christians and Churches of all faiths all over the world consider the
major problems of our day."[4] If theology is always a question of
reflecting upon faith, the type of theology wanted today is not

[3] Cf. Harvey Cox, "The Reaction of a Post-Ecumenical Christianity",
in *The Ecumenist* (Jan.–Feb. 1968), p. 119.

[4] Hans-Ruedi Weber, in his memorable address at the closing of the
Lay Apostolate Congress in Rome in 1967: Congress proceedings, vol. I
(Rome, 1968), p. 128; cf., too, p. 131. See, too, note 6, *infra*, R. McAfee
Brown, and A. H. van Heuvel, former secretary of the Department of
Youth of the W.C.C.: *The Humiliation of the Church* (London, 1967).

so much the working out of this or that dogma of tradition, as the search for a Christian understanding of the concrete experience of events and our encounter with other people. God reveals himself to us and calls us to him through men who are our brothers, and through the situations we meet in the world. This form of reflection has no need to consult any magisterium; what it is seeking is rather comparison with the reflections of other people through something more like a family conclave. This is all the more so in that the magisterium, when it comes to these particular problems, is disastrously beside the point in any answers it is asked to give. There is here an obvious danger of seeing Christian realities only in their relevance *for man*—what we may call "horizontalism".

4. Though God and the Christian mysteries as entities in themselves may be of little interest, the Church as an entity in itself is definitely under fire. If Christ is, in Bonhoeffer's splendid phrase, "the man who exists for others", people also want a Church existing for others. It seems to the more impatient as though the Church's existence for itself is such as to prevent its doing so. They see the Church's life *ad extra* as of far greater importance than its life *ad intra*; the only point of the latter is in its bearing on the presence of Christians in the world, and their evangelical oneness with all mankind. Thus there has come into being a new kind of Church altogether, separate from the structures and institutions of the old one (sometimes contemptuously labelled the "shop"). You cannot, they say, consider either the Church or ecumenism as an end in itself. You can only pray and work *for* unity. But unity, as we can see, is to be found in the common service of others, in joining together to make certain options and take certain steps towards justice, for the poor, against all forms of oppression. A Church "existing for others" and a theology of secular problems are complementary. The Church as an entity in itself has only lived and could only survive through a very special, basically clerical, medieval culture, dating from the days of the clerks and scholastics to whom, though they fought against it, one must in one sense liken the theology and the Church created by the Reformers: their theology and their Church belong to the same world—to an entity existing in and for itself, and a whole cultural world we have long since

outgrown. Here again, post-ecumenism will refer to Bonhoeffer, who feared that the Confessing Church would be content to stand firm on an intra-ecclesiastical line, and believe itself "intact" as long as it was not attacked from within its own sphere. Bonhoeffer also attacked Barth, who was after all still a cleric, for his "positivism of Revelation".[5]

II. A Positive Direction

An over-assured intellectualism on my part, and an old-fashioned pragmatism in some of the Protestant formulations of the time, led me in 1937 to fail to grasp the value and promise in the movement of practical Christianity (Life and Work). Since we have been working together to serve the world in the name of the justice of the covenant and the charity of Christ, it has become clear to me that this is a most effective way towards unity, and unity even at the theological level. As Karl Rahner said after hearing a lecture by Robert McAfee Brown, "the theological questions that divide the Christian Churches cannot be resolved by sterile debates in the style of traditional controversy. They can only be resolved if theologians concentrate their attention on the present and future, and try to re-think and preach the traditional Gospel message of God, Christ and grace, in such a way as to make it understood and accepted by the pagan of today. If the theologians of all the Churches could manage to make the Gospel real *now*, they would be preaching the same message, for they would be giving the same answer to the situation which they are all experiencing. . . ."[6] Call it "secular ecumenism" if you like.[7] Yet that is a term which can be interpreted

[5] See the letters of 30 April, 5 May and 8 June 1944, in *Letters and Papers from Prison* (Fontana edition, pp. 90, 94, 106), London, 1959.

[6] *Theology Digest* (winter 1967), p. 272. Robert McAfee Brown's lecture, "Ecumenism and the Secular Order", is in the same issue, pp. 259–71. Compare with Karl Rahner, "The Task of Theology after the Council", in *Vatican II: An Interfaith Appraisal* (Notre Dame, 1966), p. 596: "Christian theology for today's pagan is the best ecumenical theology."

[7] Mgr J. Willebrands, "Le mouvement oecuménique et la sécularisation du monde", in *Proche Orient chrétien*, 17 (1967), pp. 113–25 (which was reproduced with minor alterations in *Oecuménisme et problèmes actuels* (Paris, 1969), pp. 69–89).

in a sense I should not accept, and we must be very careful in our choice of terms, for they always have a context, and can bring with them a kind of parasite growth of ideas which alter the meaning they originally had for us. An adjective can in fact devour its noun. I should therefore prefer to speak of ecumenism for the service of all, or of commitment, or simply of working together.

It is essential that we respect the Church *as* an entity in itself—in other words, the fact that it has a life of its own—but also recognize that it exists for the sake of man, and in that sense, for the world. A healthy life, for the Church, means carrying out its mission, and allowing the world to determine how it must do it. Its future is to be present to the world's future. In that sense, a total ecumenism of common service will save theological ecumenism from turning into a sterile talk-shop among ivory-tower dwellers; it will also save institutional ecumenism from being merely a series of demonstrations leading nowhere; and spiritual ecumenism from becoming a slightly enlarged kind of closeness, an experience that warms those who share it, but radiates no heat to anyone else.

How far, though, will the general situation of secularism, and our working together to consider the genuine questions the world is asking, make possible the continuance of the kind of theological talking-points which have for centuries provided matter for our debates and, for the last forty years, for our dialogues?

A study of history, which by casting light on them can smooth over so many of the disputes we have inherited from the past, makes it very clear that such disputes date from a time when only those with deep theological knowledge had any say. Nowadays people do not accept that kind of hegemony, either because the methods and ways of thinking the theologians used now seem outmoded, or because culture has changed and become more widespread, or because the past appears linked to a whole world of middle-class values now being brought into question, or finally perhaps because other charismata seem just as important in expressing Christian fidelity.

It is obvious that, to the extent to which this kind of theological debate did deal with real problems relating to vital points in the interpretation of doctrine, our new understanding of things makes it neither more nor less important than it ever was. It remains, however, that the vastness, the urgency, the radical nature of the problems presented to the faith through the secularization of our culture—one can after all speak even of a cultural death of God—have made a decisive change in the scale of values by which we judge differences of belief. But the Christians of today who are most thoroughly committed *as Christians* to the life and work of the world of man (the *Oikumene*—the whole inhabited world) tell us that they are simply never faced with the kind of theological problems with which our theologians were grappling from the eleventh to the sixteenth centuries. To the young Churches, all that is "pre-history", and essentially European or Western—nothing to do with them at all. The faithful have a sense of having got beyond it all. To see how people's minds are moving, one may well wonder whether we shall not eventually arrive at a situation in which the kind of theological points we are discussing now will be of interest to absolutely no one. I am reminded of what Paul Claudel said of himself: having been suddenly converted on Christmas Day 1886, he did not actually practise his religion for several years, and of those years he wrote: "My philosophical convictions were total, and God scornfully left them where they were, so that I saw nothing in them to change; the Catholic religion still seemed to me the same collection of absurd legends, its priests and faithful still inspired in me the same dislike, a dislike verging on hatred and disgust. The whole structure of my opinions and my knowledge remained standing, and I saw no fault in it. That only happened once I stepped outside it."

In brief, post-ecumenism is essentially a post-ecumenism of *belief*. It is the beginning of a new chapter; those relating to confessionalism and ecclesiological controversy are finished. But in this it is simply living up more fully to what the ecumenical movement has essentially been from the first, the notion contained in its very title: *Oikoumene*, the whole world. With this difference, that it has returned to that notion after two decisive experiences which Catholics as well as the rest have been through within the life of their own Church: (1) the experience of returning to the sources, especially the Bible, leaving aside all strictly confessional positions (though without thereby rejecting them); (2) the experience of the fact that *the same questions* which the world is asking today through all its tragic tensions and its secularism face us all, and that since we all have the *same* origin, we are led to give the *same* answers and adopt the *same* commitments. Not everyone will agree on all points, but the differences will no longer be differences among the Churches, but differences among Christians within each Church. They thus tend to face us with the further problem of ecumenism among Catholics or among Protestants. . . .

III. Is Ecumenism Unnecessary?

One cannot but welcome everything positively valuable in the ecumenism of working together. Is it right to deplore a detailed examination of dogma that gives no thought to action? The young are not misguided in their dislike of those continuing debates among Christians which have no bearing on their responsibility in the world; they think there has been altogether too much said in words, and they want to speak through action. If ecumenism stops short at words, demonstrations, little academic groups congratulating one another, then we shall not achieve any entry into post-ecumenism. But if we actually examine the various traditional forms of ecumenism and consider their possibilities, we cannot throw them out lock, stock and barrel. We might glance at them briefly here.

Theological ecumenism has achieved very positive results in only thirty years. Indeed, its very achievement has made it possible for us now to see beyond it. Thanks to it, we are no longer still arguing about, for instance, tradition, justification by faith, the good intentions of the Reformers, the visibility of the Church, liturgy; and where the Orthodox are concerned, we no longer battle over the role of the Eucharist, the Fathers, the local Churches, possibly not even the procession of the Holy Spirit. And in matters exegetical, we have reached agreement on innumerable points. It seems to me certain—and not nearly widely enough recognized—that to give up exploring theological questions would amount to wrecking the chances of a reunion with Orthodoxy; it would also mean accepting an outlook of non-culture, a *diminutio capitis*, of which some people unfortunately do not even see the danger.

Undoubtedly theology has an enormous labour ahead of it if it is to express the Gospel in a new language, within a continually changing (and indeed exploding) culture. It must also develop a theology of work in the world, an ethics of development, of profound and rapid change ("revolution"), an understanding of man that is on a level with modern human knowledge, and so on. But it must also remain in line with our secular commitments, for ever demanding and criticizing, watching over the slogans and fashions of every age; it must have enough vitality of its own to exercise a critical function *et intra et extra*.

Spiritual ecumenism has been perhaps most effective of all. It is understandable that people feel a certain lassitude at the thought of celebrating a world-wide "Unity Octave" for the *nth* time. All prayer is subject to that temptation. But the practice of spiritual ecumenism is vital in giving our joint commitment to the world its true quality and depth. Unity is a grace, and ecumenism is a vast working out of grace. Prayer is indispensable for any appreciation of its real nature.

Institutional ecumenism would be pointless if it did not complement and serve the other forms of ecumenism. One cannot rest content with organizations and programmes. Something must actually happen. The institutions exist in order to be continually outgrown; they are services. But what would ecumenism be without the services of the W.C.C. or the Roman secretariat? Its whole existence would be at stake, and we must be very clear what we mean and imply when we say that.

IV. Beyond Ecumenism?

The twentieth century is both the century of ecumenism and the century of the Church, for the two are linked. To say that we have got beyond ecumenism would mean saying that the ecclesiological problem no longer exists. This might mean one of two things: either we would have decided it was resolved because substantially we are in agreement,[8] or the whole idea of

[8] In Amsterdam in 1948, W. A. Visser 't Hooft said very rightly: "If there were an ecclesiology acceptable to everyone, the ecumenical problem

the Church would be seen as an empty shell no longer of any value. This latter may be in fact the danger today. Surely to reject ecumenism indicates a crisis in ecclesiological awareness? It may look like the ramblings of an old man, but I cannot stop harping on the danger, evident in so many different movements of thought, of failing to see that the Church and the world are not the same thing. The Church arose out of, and lives by, actions of God's which cannot be lumped together with the act of creation, or the immanent history of the world. It is true that there is also a danger of seeing them as being too separate; not for nothing has the ecumenical movement continually studied the relationship between creation and redemption.[9] I myself will always set my face against any insubstantial, unreal, so-called "supernatural" conception of "salvation": it is *creation* that is saved, gathered together into the kingdom of God. Père de Lubac has clearly analysed the historical path which so unfortunately led to the falsification of the very notion of the "supernatural". It is precisely this, in combination with a lively awareness of mission, that makes it possible to believe in the Church having a healthy form of "existence in itself" that is in no way detrimental to its existing "for mankind". On the other hand, there are ways in which that "for the world" can be interpreted exclusively in terms of social revolution and human advancement, so that the Church is in danger of being reduced to no more than the inspiration for such advancement—merely, in Willebrands' phrase, "a work team".

To this one must add another interesting and disturbing tendency: to rest content with satisfying one's own conscience, with joining into communities on the basis of shared human options and commitments, without paying much heed to the normative *fact* of the institution. It is true that, in the past, especially in thematized and systematized theology, too much stress has been laid on the institutional principle. Vatican II, fortunately,

---

would be resolved, and the ecumenical 'movement' unnecessary"; in "Qu'est-ce que le Conseil oecuménique des Eglises", *Desordre de l'Homme et Dessein de Dieu*, I, p. 264.

[9] We may recall the fine statement by Dean J. Sittler in New Delhi in 1961, "Called to Unity" (text in *The Ecumenist* (Feb.–Jan. 1962), pp. 177–87).

condemned legalism, rediscovered charismata, sanctioned a liturgy of participation, and returned to the old idea of the importance of local Churches. I think there still remains a lot to do if the principle of the individual is to be given its true value. The Church makes us, but we make the Church; the Eucharist makes the Church, but the Church makes the Eucharist. We must no more see *exclusively* the first aspect than the second. I do not know if I am wrong, but it seems to me that this statement casts light on the problem of inter-communion and inter-celebration with which the post-ecumenical period faces us. If dogmatic differences are pre-history seen now as of little interest, if unity is primarily a matter of agreement as to this world's options and commitments to human advancement, if faith is primarily an interpretation of life, and mission a confrontation between that faith and the experience of other people and events, then it is perfectly natural to express the kind of brotherhood that results from them by sharing the bread of the Eucharist. But the Eucharist is then no longer the act *of the Church*, and indeed the Church has been forgotten. Though it has enormous value, such a position ultimately represents a reduction of everything to the merely human.

There is a similar question from the point of view of our mission. The ecumenism that consists in providing similar, if not identical, answers to the great problems of the world, is not the sum total of the mission we have received from Christ and his apostles. This latter also, and indeed more importantly, includes a design to convert men to the faith, and make them part of the people God wants to create for himself in the world. Now this can only be achieved by joining one of the Churches that are at present divided. It is true that in the long term, our practice of "post-ecumenism" will change the elements of this thorny problem.[10] One may even wonder whether a kind of "missionary post-activity" is not here and there tending to replace missionary activity proper. However, unless we are to yield to that tendency

---

[10] "Secular ecumenism" would sympathize with the idea that God is already acting in the world; the Church's job is not so much to bring it what it has not got, as to recognize what it has already got, revealing it by its true name, and giving thanks. See, for instance, A. H. van den Heuvel, *op. cit.*, n. 4, *supra*.

—which would surely be a betrayal—unless we are to admit, at least for the moment, a kind of pooled mission of all the Churches, the mission we have from Christ and the apostles must resist the establishment of any pure "post-ecumenism". If the Churches remain where they are, with the Catholic Church as legitimate, then we certainly still have good reason to preserve pure and simple ecumenism, ecumenism among the Churches.

If the Church is to remain the Church, I think that ecumenism is neither unnecessary, nor something we have got beyond. It is simply that we must pursue it to the full, every aspect of it being necessary if it is to attain to all truth. This does not mean that we should stop inventing, trying new initiatives, opening new possibilities. I would even agree that post-ecumenism, with its criticism, its demands and indeed its impatience, can have an extremely beneficial effect on ecumenism as a whole. It will certainly prevent its turning into any kind of sterile Church-centredness.

Translated by Rosemary Middleton

Nikos Nissiotis

What Still Separates Us from the Catholic Church?
1. An Orthodox Reply

THE question we are faced with is a delicate and complex one; it becomes more complex still if one makes an attempt in this day and age to answer it from a confessional, and particularly, an Orthodox, standpoint. Any answer, in fact, must take account, first, of the historical, political and psychological causes that exist alongside the purely theological ones, and second, of the enormously rapid modifications and developments within Roman Catholicism since Vatican II. In other words, we can no longer simply produce a comparative theology in which we list differences of belief, nor can we express our divergences solely on the basis of statements contained in dogmatic textbooks. In addition, it is indubitably a fact that the ethos of ecumenism is leading us —even perhaps unconsciously—to adopt an entirely new kind of openness towards the other Churches; we are being forced to make an effort to reinterpret our differences of belief in the light of the present tendency of all separated Christians to come together. I therefore propose to divide my answer into three sections: first, the question of belief pure and simple; then the nature of the changes that have taken place within Roman Catholicism during and since Vatican II; and finally, what we may hope for in the future on the basis of those changes.

I. DIFFERENCES OF BELIEF BETWEEN ROME AND THE EASTERN CHURCH

Before considering those differences, I should like to make a comment on the title of this article. The editors of *Concilium* asked me to answer this question: *Was trennt uns immer noch von der katholischen Kirche?* "What still separates us from the Catholic Church?"

I realize that in the West you use the term "Catholic Church" to mean the Church of Rome. But phrased thus, the question is in danger of stressing what is in fact the most controversial point of all between Rome and the other Churches—above all, the Orthodox. For the Orthodox Church remains firmly convinced that it has never in fact been separated from the one, Catholic and apostolic Church, but is in faithful and unbroken continuity with it, both historically and ecclesiologically. Furthermore, the Orthodox consciousness will never admit that there is any evidence in history to indicate that the Orthodox Church broke away from the Roman Church. The history of the Church in the first ten centuries, as taught by Eastern historians, leads the Orthodox to believe that it was the Roman Church which broke away from Orthodoxy, and must therefore bear the major responsibility for the schism between the two.

This appears to me a vital point on which we must dwell, for where such attitudes prevail dogmatic discussion can only take place in an atmosphere of extreme and mutual exclusivism. The result is that the theological debate between Rome and Orthodoxy, however close the two Churches may be at the ecclesiological level, becomes more difficult than either body's debate with any of the reformed Churches, different though these may be ecclesiologically.

From the very first, there have existed divergences of theology in Christianity. The nature and structure of the Church were differently understood in East and West, because of the differing cultural and political outlook in each, inherited one from Greece, the other from Rome. I have no wish to exaggerate those differences, but one is forced by the facts to recognize that the problem of the authority of the hierarchy in the Church—which was to be the major cause of the schism after the eighth century—was understood and applied very differently in the two areas.

Though the dogma of the papacy could be given an ecclesiological or biblical basis, it was not a dogma that the Orthodox saw as flowing naturally from the development of either the history or the teaching of the Church; it seemed far more the result of historical events illustrating Rome's fervent desire (a desire no doubt based on the most excellent intentions on the part of the popes and bishops of the time) to give the Church an additional form of unity, a more solid and efficient basis, which they saw as being entirely and unquestionably for its good. This is a simple fact; and it would not be easy at this late date to alter the view of the Orthodox that the origins of the schism lay primarily in Rome's wish to dominate the East, with papal primacy and infallibility being introduced simply as an *a posteriori* justification for doing so.

As time went on, various new interpretations of dogma and innovations in liturgical practice were simply so many further proofs to the Orthodox of this position of power adopted by Rome. It was in fact Rome alone that decided to add the *filioque* to the Nicene creed, thus showing a complete lack of respect for conciliarity in the Church and the ecumenical synods. To the Orthodox, therefore, it was not different theological concepts of the Holy Spirit which led to the schism, but rather Rome's way of acting unilaterally, and without any prior discussions with the Churches of the East, on a matter which affected the belief of the entire Church.

In this, Rome indicated an isolationism, an exclusivism, which destroyed the bonds of love and mutual respect between the two traditions, and made it all too likely that they would gradually grow further and further apart.

In regard to the *filioque*, indeed, it certainly would be possible to reach a far closer position theologically. This, at least, seems to be the view of Western theologians, and in the East too there are authors whose theological positions would virtually identify the eternal fact of the Holy Spirit's proceeding from the Father with the sending of the Spirit by Christ in time.[1] Indeed, it may be that the absolute unity of the three persons in the Trinity means that there can be no radical separation between the procession and mission of the Spirit, and forces us to admit that Christ shares from all eternity in "every act done by the Father in order to save

[1] See *L'Esprit Saint et l'Eglise* (Paris, 1969): the article by M. Le Guillou, "Réflexions sur la théologie des Pères Grecs en rapport avec le *filioque*", pp. 195–220.

the world".[2] But, on the other hand, for an Orthodox to affirm this must not involve appealing to any absolute and logical system of identity, for, according to the Bible, it is the very distinction between procession and mission that preserves the distinction among the three persons. Eastern theologians, faithful to their biblical roots, and anxious to be precise on this particular point (John 15. 26), prefer to say that the Holy Spirit proceeds *eternally* from the Father, and is sent by the Son *in time*. The earliest theology and tradition make it hard to adopt any other view, yet it was this tradition that Rome decided unilaterally to alter.

Other ways in which Rome has deviated from early tradition will similarly be held by the Orthodox to be authoritarian and unilateral decisions made in disregard of conciliarity as a method of exercising authority; thus they force us to face the whole problem of the papacy—not just the problem of papal primacy and its function in assuring the unity of the Church, but of the papacy itself as a dogma preceding, qualifying and manipulating other dogmas and practices of the universal Church. The Orthodox have never denied that there is a genuine primacy of love and honour due to the Bishop of Rome;[3] but to them it is precisely as bishop of Rome, and not as some kind of universal super-bishop, wielding a supreme juridical authority as successor to Peter and Vicar of Christ.[4] The primacy of love is something far deeper, more spiritual and more charismatic than any legalistic primacy of jurisdiction. It is the true primacy, and finds its justification in the awareness of the faithful rather than in any antiquated theology of identification with the person of Peter. For it is that identification that leads to a belief in the individual infallibility of the Pope, instead of in the communal infallibility existing in the mind of the whole Church.

If the papacy is not seen within the framework of the authority

---

[2] See *Le Saint Esprit* (Geneva, 1963): the article by G. Widmer, "Saint Esprit et Théologie trinitaire", pp. 107–29.

[3] See *La Primauté de Pierre dans l'Eglise Orthodoxe* (Neuchâtel, 1960), by N. Afanassieff, N. Koulounzine, J. Meyendorff and A. Schemann.

[4] This was clearly expressed by Vatican II in the Dogmatic Constitution on the Church, para. 22: "In effect, the Roman Pontiff, in virtue of his office as Vicar of Christ and Pastor of the whole Church, has full power, a supreme and universal power over the Church. And he can always exercise this power freely"; see also para. 24 and para. 25, etc.

of the People of God whose servant it is, then all kinds of errors will follow, causing continual disharmony within the Church. The disproportionate qualitative difference between hierarchy and People,[5] communion under only one kind, enforced clerical celibacy, the publication of encyclicals that run completely counter to the wishes of the People—all these things become possible. Certainly the administration of the Church functions better under the juridical and monarchical authority of the papacy, but at every moment there is a corresponding danger that the problem of that authority will occur to the minds of her members. And it further creates confusion in regard to the supreme norms of truth, and how these are to be expressed.

Obviously the tradition of the papacy has been a tremendous factor for unity in Catholicism, and the Orthodox should value that aspect of it; but at the same time it constitutes a direct and permanent danger to that unity, since the People of God want to give expression to their own authentic understanding, so as to help towards the renewal of the Church and her presence in the world. When that happens, this same papacy can give rise to dissensions, schisms and breakaway movements in the Church.

What divides the Eastern Churches from Rome as they see it, and in the light of their understanding of Church history, is therefore first and foremost Rome's own attitude, which endows a monarchical administration with primacy over the People of God, and thus sets up a geographical and ecclesiological centre above the local Churches, and overshadows the local bishops with a super-bishop.[6]

This deviation is then justified by a series of theological interpretations which further accentuate the centralization of power in the Roman Church. Around that individual geographical centre, there then forms a circle closed in upon itself. Between

[5] *Ibid.*, paras. 37 and 36, which indicate that despite the considerable effort made at Vatican II to eliminate this over-rigid distinction from the past, certain texts reaffirm it and make it very apparent to Orthodox eyes.

[6] *Ibid.*, para. 22, where we read, among other remarks: "The order of Bishops ... is also, together with its head the Roman Pontiff, and never without this head, the subject of supreme and full power over the universal Church, a power that can be exercised only with the consent of the Roman Pontiff."

the Pope and the bishops, they have introduced a further super-
fluous rank, unknown in the early Church, the Cardinalate, thus
endangering the entire charismatic structure of the Church. So,
alongside the problem of authority within the Church, we find
the problem arising of authority in relation to the world and the
State—the secular power; and this means that Rome, if it is to
remain completely autonomous in every area, must either declare
itself as having some kind of stateless status, or become a State
in its own right.

It is at this point that we find the greatest difficulty of all between Roman and Orthodox: a universalist and centralist system
confronts an autonomous system of local Churches, based on a
synodal and conciliar administration. The Orthodox are aware
that there is no one ideal solution, and fully recognize the practical problems existing in their own system. But it is that system
that separates them from Rome, or rather that makes them see
Rome as having taken a road which separates it from the
Churches of the East. All Rome's superior organization, effi-
ciency and administrative advantages will not serve to convince
the Orthodox of the theoretical and practical value of Rome's
system. To them, it is a matter of faith and fidelity, and it is precisely from that supremacy as against the world, and that pyra-
midal form of unity with a single summit, that they want to
preserve their Church.

II. THE CHANGES WROUGHT BY VATICAN II

The Orthodox do not in fact fully realize what has happened
inside the Catholic Church since Vatican II. In their own Church,
they have experienced no profound inner change which has tem-
porarily shaken it to its roots. Yet it is just that that happened to
the Roman Church at the Council, and has been going on, gradually and continuously, since it opened up to the present time. The
Orthodox should not consider only the theological aspects of
Vatican II. It is true that the documents it published—with the
exception of a few modifications to suit the modern world, or
the adopting of some slightly altered theological positions—did
not appear to indicate any radical change in Roman theology on
any of the points I have mentioned above. But the Council must

not be understood only in terms of the documents it produced. It was also, and supremely, a significant *event*, and one which has transformed the whole atmosphere of the Roman Church. I should like to give here a few of the points in that transformation which are significant from an Orthodox point of view:

(*a*) The very fact of the Council; simply by being convened it provided the best possible proof of the Roman Church's desire to return to the conciliar tradition.

(*b*) The collegiality of Pope and bishops. This is perhaps an unfortunate way of expressing it, for collegiality is an integral part of the notion of the whole People of God. On the other hand, alongside texts stating that collegiality as clearly as possible, there are others confirming papal primacy. None the less, the fact remains that that traditional primacy has been rocked to its foundations by a General Council of the Roman Church.

(*c*) The idea of the People of God has been re-emphasized, and set before the notion of hierarchy; and this makes it possible for us to hope for a new ecclesiological interpretation of the meaning of the *pleroma*.

(*d*) The Eastern Church has been recognized at the highest level *as a Church* and placed on the same ecclesiological level as Rome; furthermore, the other Churches, and the whole ecumenical movement, have been defined positively as being the fruit of the Holy Spirit at work.

(*e*) The Roman Church has been seen to criticize itself publicly, and has not shrunk from going through a crisis of authority in full view of the outside world—a crisis involving precisely that element which has up to now constituted its strength and its backbone. Finally, and most important, is the fact that the Council has marked the beginning of a move towards a transformation —a transformation illustrated abundantly by things which have happened since. Eminent bishops make statements.[7] Theologians

[7] See Cardinal Suenens' interview of May 1969 (published in English in *The Tablet*). Among other things, he says: "Christ entrusted his Church to Peter and the Eleven, who are diversely but indissolubly linked in a twofold way: there was the link between the Eleven and Peter, and the link between Peter and both the Eleven and the people of God." Later, he says: "[The Bishop] must accept a new method of exercising his authority...by making use of the more democratic methods explicitly demanded by the Council." And also: "[The Pope] is at once Bishop of

interpret them by outlining a wholly new picture of the Pope and the Roman Church and its attempts to de-centralize and de-absolutize its monarchy.[8] The kind of renewal taking place in the Roman Church now is such as will make it possible to open wider doors to a dialogue with the East in the future.

What is quite specially noteworthy is the enormous flexibility achieved by the Roman Catholic world in general—bishops, priests, laity, the young—during the time since the Council. At this moment all the points that have traditionally divided Rome and Orthodoxy have been brought into question. It is true that in most cases, especially where biblical theology, hermeneutics and exegesis are concerned, it is the theology of the Reformation with which Catholics are making their comparisons. This is natural enough, for there has long been a dialogue between the two theologies. Still, in addition to such obvious and understandable affinities, what has been happening among Catholics since the Council also has tremendous bearing upon a whole ecclesiological reform in the direction of adopting an administrative system which will give far more importance to the local Churches. Such a reform could, in practice, throw into relief the collegiality which was formulated, even if not wholly clearly, by the Council. After all, it has always been the life of the Church that has qualified and interpreted—by its way of carrying them out—the ambiguous decisions of Councils.

There is one particularly hopeful element in the present debate

---

Rome, Archbishop and Metropolitan of the Roman province, Primate of Italy, Patriarch of the West, Head of the universal Church, and also Head of the Vatican State." The question is: "Out of all these, which are of divine law, which merely historical accident?" This is also the question which the Orthodox are asking. And it is fairly clear that the two latter functions belong to historical accident alone, and not to the life of the one true Church of West and East.

[8] See "Portrait d'un Pape", by Hans Küng, Le Monde, 12 August 1969. He writes: "Such a Pope would be imbued with an authentically evangelical concept of the Church, not with a juridical, formalistic, static and bureaucratic notion of it, nor yet one of it as a centralized unit of administration with the bishops as no more than the Pope's delegates or instruments, but as a Church whose authentic expression is in the local Churches. . . ." That is precisely the direction which the Orthodox Church would hope to see any change in the understanding and practice of the papacy taking.

over centralism in Rome, and that is that the contestants, theologians and priests, are faithful Catholics, with no intention of leaving their Church or dividing it up into other Churches. Their loyalty to their Church is at no point in doubt, despite the violence of the debate. This absolute fidelity makes the present Catholic debate a most valuable one in Orthodox eyes, for the one thing the Orthodox can never admit is for the Church to be continually fragmented by the movements of renewal within it.

III. Towards a Happier Future

This new climate makes it justifiable for us to hope for a new situation in the future. Indeed it was that conciliar atmosphere that made it possible for the Pope and the Patriarch of Constantinople to meet three times in three years, and most important of all, to lift the anathemas pronounced in 1054. In theory, once the anathemas were lifted, communion between the two Churches should have been re-established, for it was they, rather than differences in theology, which actually destroyed the communion. Evidently, then, we are faced here with psychological obstacles making it impossible for either of us at present to consider the "other" Church as "ours". We have to learn to have confidence in a form of church structure different from our own; and finally, through communion, we must strengthen our steps towards re-establishing organic union. That will demand effort on both sides. Not only must the Pope enter into real collegiality with his bishops, but he must modify his supreme right to sanction the ordination of every individual to the episcopate from his position as "head of the bishops".

As for the Orthodox, they too must take a critical look at themselves, and try to rid themselves of any form of verbal and theoretical triumphalism. They will have to endeavour to understand that certain aspects of the Roman faith are not as negative as they appear, and may even have a major part to play in the achievement of unity. If the papacy is valued in the right way, and stripped of its exclusivism, it could well, as a primacy of love, become a great charismatic force for unity. Thus, the question I have been asked: "What separates us from the Catholic Church?" cannot be answered simply in terms of the problems Rome presents to Orthodoxy. We too must change, must be renewed, must rid ourselves of prejudices and of our "allergy" against the papacy. We must consciously recognize the possibility of things being different in the future, of events occurring which may alter certain elements in any Church's life. Today, above all, the spread of ecumenism and Rome's new attitude to it, should lead us to admit that there is a new spirit abroad in the relationships among all the Churches, and especially between Rome and the East— and that admission should stir us from our attitude of indifference and pessimism. Facing the future with confidence, and ceasing to harp on past divisions and blame them solely on the Latins' need to dominate, we must give full recognition to the value of the changes going on at this moment.

There are a great many ways in which we could be coming closer even now; many things that make us aware that what separates us need not actually hamper our movements, nor force us to remain out of communion with one another.

I should like to make three comments in this regard:

(a) It is no use expecting the concept of the papacy to change quickly or easily to an image of the Pope comparable with our image of an Eastern Patriarch as *primus inter pares* in our sense. We must understand and accept the fact that papal primacy has, over the course of the Western Church's history, become a constitutive element in Roman Catholicism. What we must decide is whether we cannot still move towards communion, while accepting that that primacy is an internal affair of the Roman Church. As long as Rome does not force it upon the other Churches, it can remain merely a problem for her own people, to the extent that they themselves decide to accept or reject it. There are visible signs of change within Roman Catholicism, so it is evidently not a matter of having to reform Rome before we can take any steps towards re-unification. The first step is coexistence, in an effort to understand each other better, and help each other to a better understanding of the points on which we differ, especially as regards the notion of authority in the Church, and its function in the present-day world.

(b) The present development of relations between the Roman

and Orthodox Churches is due to the earlier development of the ecumenical movement, and especially to the achievements of the World Council of Churches. It was not by chance that the first contacts between our two Churches took place within the ecumenical movement. That is why it is vital that every effort they make to draw closer must keep in mind all the other Churches involved in the movement. Rome and Orthodoxy cannot let themselves form a little Catholic enclave so that their full recognition of each other will end up by accentuating the differences between them and all the rest—whether Anglican or Protestant. If, on the purely dogmatic level, what divides the Catholics of Rome from those of the East is not so serious, then both groups should be encouraged, and fully and sincerely committed together to the ecumenical movement; we should be ready to work together in all humility for the unity of the whole Church. After all, between us, we do not constitute the whole of Christianity, and while we draw closer, we still need the presence and goodwill of the other Churches; we must be careful never to forget what our own renewal owes to the challenge—and the vision—provided by the rest. Thus, the drawing together of Orthodoxy and Roman Catholicism is an integral part of the whole ecumenical movement—as indeed is the case with every other movement towards unity between Churches.

(c) Finally, when trying to answer the question asked in our title, we cannot leave aside the problem of the Uniates, which is a very sensitive one to the Orthodox. There are even some of us for whom Uniatism forms the gravest of all obstacles on the path to union between Rome and Orthodoxy. For the little Uniate Churches, living among the Orthodox, yet recognized by Rome as part of its Body, are a proof that acceptance of the primacy of Rome is all that is needed to make Rome recognize break-away groups of Orthodox as valid and canonical. For, in fact, such communities largely exist because of Roman proselytizing among the Orthodox; apparently, according to Roman Canon Law, the Orthodox have only to accept papal primacy to become members of the one true Church, while in all other respects preserving the whole theological and liturgical tradition of the East.

It would be false to pretend that the present state of affairs with the Uniate Churches is not difficult in the extreme for both groups, especially the Orthodox. But this problem must not be allowed to paralyse our efforts to draw together, nor serve as an excuse for doing nothing when we ought to be working for reconciliation. And the Uniates may not be wholly wrong in thinking that they in fact serve the cause of mediating between Rome and Orthodoxy, even though nowadays our direct relations have improved so enormously. During the Council, the Uniates, from within the Catholic body, openly criticized various ecclesiological attitudes in the Latin Church. Furthermore, we Orthodox who want to work for unity with Rome must not forget that it is precisely in regard to those points which up to now we have seen in a wholly negative light, that we must try to recognize the positively good elements. Instead of considering the Uniates as apostates, it would be more helpful to see them as yet one more means towards dialogue. Through this new access-road, and with this new vision of our task before God, we shall truly become workers for unity. For what is needed above all is a change of mind and heart, not just of externals. The truth cannot be understood and lived in unity among the Churches unless there is a spirit of mutual understanding; then what seems impossible to man will be achieved in God.

Thus, from the Orthodox standpoint, the question, "What separates us from the Roman Catholic Church?" can be given diametrically opposite answers. On the one hand, one may adopt a negative position, on the basis of comparative theology, and go on to justify one's attitude by the events of history, and deny the possibility of Rome's ever changing in the future: this would mean seeing only the negative side of Roman Catholicism. On the other hand, one may work out one's answer by getting beyond those negative aspects and recognizing the rapid changes Roman Catholicism is undergoing in the world at this moment, thus opening whole new perspectives of understanding and action. It is this second attitude I have opted for in my attempt to answer the question. Though fully aware of the difficulties, I have tried to see the problem in the light of what is taking place *now* in the Roman Church, with the added understanding given by the evident development of the ecumenical movement. The historical fact of ecumenism is so obvious and so immediate as to enable us to discover a whole new horizon, which calls us forward to a new commitment, and gives us new hope in the God whose will is that we all be reunited in his one Church, for the service of all mankind; for mankind will only find its unity as a single human family in and through that one true Church. The reunion between Western and Eastern Christians may be seen as a starting-point for the whole unity of mankind. Along that road, to the union of East and West, the first indispensable step is the re-establishment of ecclesial and eucharistic communion between Rome and Orthodoxy. And it is a step that could be possible in the near future.

Translated by Rosemary Middleton

Kristen Skydsgaard

What Still Separates Us from the Catholic Church?
2. A Protestant Reply

I. An Ambiguous Situation

I HAVE to answer the question as a representative of the Protestant tradition which derives from the most extensive break in the Christian Church—the Lutheran Reformation. It's not an easy task. The rift had effects so far-reaching that right up to the present the word "Reformation" has seemed to Catholics to stand for something very dangerous and even odious—a reaction that even now has not wholly disappeared. The same is true of the Protestant attitude to the word "Catholic", which was and to some extent is a pejorative term.

What was the Reformation? History offers a great number of contradictory answers that need no enumeration here. It is enough to remark that the Reformation was concerned with the essence of Christian belief: the divinity of God, the justification of sinners, and faith in Christ; the nature of the Christian Church, the primacy of Holy Writ, and the proclamation of the Gospel—in short, with man's salvation. He who said No simultaneously said Yes to the one, holy, catholic and apostolic Church; and said it clearly and unequivocally. Had this not been the case, ultimately the Reformation would have no significance, except, perhaps, as a milestone on the route of human history; in Christian terms it would be just a tragic event. But the Reformation was significant for the *whole* Church; its purpose was not to establish a special Lutheran Church, but to renew the Church of God.

The rift is still between us. There are Catholics and Protestants who are convinced that the break is definitive, and the situation an Either-Or. Much (they would admit) has changed in the course of time. The Second Vatican Council is important, but its importance ought not to be pressed too far on the other side. For (they would object) despite all the reforms, despite the changed mentality of many Catholics, and despite the Decree on Ecumenism, *essentially* everything has stayed as it was. No dogma has been questioned: neither papal infallibility nor the two most recent Marian pronouncements. Trent—that negative answer to the Reformation—is still effective.

On the Catholic side, too, there are those who say that the significance of the Council must not be over-emphasized, and that each particular must be interpreted according to the unmistakable tradition of the Church. On both sides there are those who, anxious for the preservation of essential truth and the perseverance of the faithful in the strait way, admonish any who would forget these points.

There are Catholics and Evangelicals who see the matter quite differently and believe we may well be already on the way to reunion. So much has already happened and so many barriers have been removed, that unity is no longer mere wishful thinking but a reality the outlines of which can already be perceived. The Roman Catholic Church would seem to have cast off its Counter-Reformation mentality. Even though its dogmas are substantially the same, the way in which we understand them is open to change: substance and mode of expression are not identical. Even the doctrine of papal infallibility could well be re-interpreted, and the Marian dogmas made part of an appropriate christology. Each Council of the Church would have to be interpreted in accordance with its particular historical perspective. Reunion is to be seen not as a kind of return but as a "homecoming" that would be a great blessing for both parties. Only when this happens can the genuine Reformed inheritance take effect in the Catholic Church.

I realize quite well that this is a very general outline; nevertheless, although reality is often more complicated, the situation is essentially one of two basically different attitudes. The "still" of the question "What still separates us from the Catholic Church?" shows that it is asked from the second of the two viewpoints I have described. I shall now concern myself with this "still" in more detail.

II. THE CHURCH ON THE MOVE

On 21 May 1931 an Austrian clerical journal carried a leading article by Dr Josef Dillersberger, a young New Testament scholar. The contribution was in the form of a fervent Pentecostal prayer for the renewal of the Catholic Church, addressed to the Holy Spirit who makes all things new: "But where are you on this earth? They say that your Church is full of the Spirit, yet everything there is so quiet, so motionless—even partly dead. 'Two-thirds corpsemeat!' was the judgment of a Soviet Communist. . . . Lord, *everything in your Church is so old!* The old counts—much more than the new. For us, an innovator is virtually a heretic. If anything new threatens in our Church there's an immediate outcry: 'Take care! Old ways are best. We've never done anything different. Why change all of a sudden?' In your Church that asks you to make all things new, ever and again that which is new meets with the greatest mistrust and rejection. . . . Spirit of the Lord, you love the new. When will you renew the face of your Church? When will you show us how much that is old in your Church should and must disappear so that its countenance may once again be new and beautiful and young? If you will it, the old will vanish in the power of your descent upon us and all will be made new. If you will it . . . already I can hear from afar the many thousands of those who do not believe, calling out with strong emotion and impressive faith: 'The old is gone—but see, the new has come to pass!' But now it is often difficult to have faith in you, Holy Spirit; and it is painful now to add a hallelujah! to the prayer that asks you to renew the earth. . . ."
". . . Let your Church be *stirred up* once more! Make *new* its countenance, and let the banner of *freedom* wave once again over the children of God."

This prayer caused a stir in itself. Dillersberger was suspended from his academic post by the papal Congregation of Studies and was fully rehabilitated only recently. Would it be too much to say that the Second Vatican Council was in many respects the fulfilment of his prayer? For centuries the Roman Catholic Church had been thought of as monolithic. *Semper eadem*—and assuredly it was so. But this very Church has begun to move, and to move with a vengeance. Before the whole world, decisively and responsibly, the Catholic Church has examined itself critically, acknowledged its weaknesses, made positive efforts to overcome its rigidity and "triumphalism" with regard to other Churches and the world, and turned to the true sources of renewal.

My title question is asked in the light of this situation. There *could* be a modicum of impatience in the asking. Is everything between us really going to stay as it was? Isn't there any reaction to what has happened and still is happening among us in theology and in practical Church affairs? In any case, the question contains an invitation to look at things not "historically" but in the situation of the present moment.

III. Vanishing Differences and the Pope's "Credo"

Is it possible to pick out definite points which still separate us? Is it possible to make a renewed examination of essentials and produce a formula to reveal clearly the real difference *today*? Are such differences necessarily of the kind that would separate Churches, or are they such that they could co-exist in the one Church as different mental structures together with their various consequences—practical ones as well?

The Roman Catholic Church became in fact another Church. And the Churches that came from the Reformation were soon seriously affected by the "monolithic" spirit. The fire from the volcano of the Reformation soon became the hardened lava of the Lutheran and Reformed establishments—although admittedly there were occasional signs of the glow far below.

Now these Churches, too, have started to move. So it seems justifiable to ask what still separates us. The matter is made difficult by the non-homogeneity of the Churches on either side. This has long been the case in the Reformed Churches. Often the

difference between the various fractions and theological and ecclesiastical directions was almost as great as that between "Evangelical" and "Catholic". Often it was sustained only by the bond of
a national Church. Today the Roman Catholic Church, too, is
not a homogeneous entity. The question "What still separates us
from the Catholic Church?" can legitimately be countered with
the question "Which Catholic Church?" Hans Küng may have
written a book called *The Church* but there are other books about
the Church! There are irreconcilable fractions and tendencies.
There is even an "underground Church" consisting mostly of
young people who are convinced that they can live as Christians
only in opposition to the official Church. It's just the same as on
the other side. Christians from both sides pass beyond the disciplinary borders of their Churches to celebrate Holy Communion
together. Is this behaviour sacrilege or the onset of that which is
new? Isn't it part of the image of the Catholic Church today?
Who can be sure that it is just a temporary phenomenon?

Today there are Catholic theologians who understand their
Evangelical colleagues better than their own. And there are Evangelical theologians who feel more at home with Catholics. There
are occasions when Catholics and Evangelicals know that they
are wholly one. They no longer think of difference—although of
course difference remains "without", on the one hand as a question of ecclesiastical law, on the other as problems that still await
solution. These and other phenomena are "eschatological signs"
of the moment. I shall return shortly to these indications of the
Church's "new start".

What still separates us from the Catholic Church? Already it
is clear that it's no easy question. Our common situation today
has displaced the simpler situation of the past. Nevertheless I
feel compelled to persist in considering the question (one actually
put to me).

At the end of the "Year of Faith", on 30 June 1968, Pope Paul
VI made a solemn declaration of faith in St Peter's. He did this
as the supreme shepherd and ultimate authority of the Church
of God on earth. I assume that the contents of the confession of
faith are known. The Pope wished to speak as fully and as clearly
as possible. He addressed himself expressly to all men who search
for truth in the world of the present.

This "credo" was certainly welcomed by many of the faithful as a necessary aid and timely warning. In the spiritual confusion of the times, the Pope had to make a clear and unequivocal declaration of Christian belief. I don't think he succeeded. It is a Christian confession of faith in so far as it is dependent on apostolic and traditional ecclesiastical symbolic language. But everything has become so complex. It is arguable that this confession of faith really belongs to a time before the Council. In any case, there is no mention in it of a hierarchy of truths. Depressed, one concludes that the Pope, disconcerted by the situation in the Roman Catholic Church, was anxiously concerned to affirm the faith of that Church in its entirety and in its traditional, conservative form, with a clear proviso against attempts to offer new interpretations of points of belief. It would have been much happier and more auspicious had the Pope concentrated on the major— the essential—issues of faith that deeply concern men of our time, and thus grappled with the doubt and questioning of countless people.

Could it be that the Christian faith has here been "religionized" in a peculiar way, because a biblical, historical and concrete dimension has been lost that was still discernible with the Reformers? This "credo" is a voice raised against a misconceived demythologization of Christian belief, and justifiably so; but it is arguable that this very declaration of faith has succumbed to a form of mythologization that distorts or veils the essential nature of Christian faith. For instance, original sin and the Real Presence seem to be presented in a way that is really no longer viable. And anyone who asks how else the Pope could have spoken in his capacity as the ultimate authority must be answered thus: "Perhaps you're right—but that precisely is the point which separates us so grievously."

The major question is whether the Pope can now really be considered as the only valid mouthpiece of the Roman Catholic Church. Does he actually represent the entire Catholic Church? If this question can be answered only with a decisive Yes, then we are certainly faced with an almost insoluble dilemma.

This brings me to the decisive point. In spite of everything, what has been said so far is not final—not even the papal "credo" and other so-called authoritative pronouncements from both sides. This does not mean that the foregoing carries no weight, but that it is *not* that which is ultimately decisive for us today. I shall have more to say about this before I close this article.

IV. THE "NEW START"

I have already used the expression "a new start" in relation to the Church. It indicates that something new is in the offing. A situation that we had got used to is no more. We must prepare for something new and be ready for a journey into the unknown. This horizon of the new unites us both, for we are faced with the same questions.

For example, we are both experiencing the transition from a metaphysical-rational and abstract to a concrete and historical mode of thought. On both sides, dogmatic theology has been hard put to it to answer the serious questions of historical exegesis, which ask whether our credal and doctrinally abstract way of conceiving and expressing the Christian faith can really stand firm. We are together in this transition to a new understanding of the reality of our existential (i.e., historical) being. The outcome is still in the future, but on both sides we can already see great changes in the theological understanding and mode of existence that have held sway until now. Our confessional and dogmatic foundations are being shaken.

But the situation is more far-ranging—more deep-reaching. We must both learn to think more biblically; more in accordance with the Old Testament. For the primitive Church, Israel was a figure of the people of God *on the way*—"wandering". Israel was the people of God that never found ultimate peace, and was never allowed a fixed and abiding resting-place, but had always to make a new start. The word of God was no fixed and inviolable entity, but a living word—the ever new. God dwelt "in dialogue" with his people, but this dialogue was no affectionate conversation, and had no organic, unbroken evolution; it was often an angry and critical encounter in which God hid his countenance. Israel was not hidden, but had repeatedly to surrender security in order to follow the paths of God. Israel was a people of exodus and exile, and as such was given to hear the word of infinitely compassionate love, which brought that which was new out of nothingness. Even though the new people of God is radically different from the old, this dimension of the "new start" applies to the Christian Church as well. It would be (and of course has been) disastrous were ecclesiology to forget this.

The full assembly of the World Council of Churches in Uppsala (1968) was led in the final prayer of the morning by some young Christians from the German Democratic Republic. These thirty minutes proved one of the most moving occasions of the whole conference. I shall quote only a few sentences, which take their keynote from Jeremiah 7. 1–15: "Lord, we have assembled in the Churches, saying, 'This is the temple of the Lord, we are safe here.' We have assembled in the Ecumenical Council of Churches, saying, 'This is the temple of the Lord, we are safe here.' Together we have settled our minor differences. We have discussed our worship and our finances. But too often we have shut ourselves off from those outside. We have not admitted the blind, the lame and the immature, but have left them alone with their problems. And now we affirm that safety within the Church has become an empty thing; that the words pronounced there are often alien to us as well, having nothing to do with our real concerns. We have wanted to keep you for ourselves, Lord, and now in our Church as well we are no longer certain of you."

For centuries, Christians and their Churches were "on top". In spite of all resistance, they were secure, "in power". The "new start" means that all that has changed. The Churches are being led into the exile of powerlessness, the powerlessness of being inconclusive. We are being led into ways where we shall see something that is not apparent in the textbooks of dogma these days. This situation is one of judgment and promise, as in the Israel of the Old Testament. It is a judgment because the Churches have to bear a heavy burden of guilt, because they left the world to itself, and because they were rich and secure *in* the world.

If God now hides himself (or to speak in the modern manner— if God is now "dead"), then it is the living God himself who "withdraws", because he would tell us that we ought not to address him and serve him in *our* way. "God dies" because he is living. This is a judgment but also a promise, because in the midst of this very darkness God would reveal his grace to us and show us his living Christ. Then the complex will be made as nothing, for everything will be awfully and mercifully simple. The theme of the Bible is: Through death to life.

Then it is possible for what now prevents us from celebrating the Eucharist together to vanish. The situation presses towards a transcending of our theological considerations. As the judged and reprieved, we *have to* approach the table of the Lord together. And despite all the walls we have erected, Christ will be with us—in the nights of exile. And won't our theological discussions be quite different *after* celebrating the Eucharist in common? The difficulties won't disappear all at once, but the dialogue will have a dimension that was not apparent beforehand. The question about what separates us, and its answer, will be different from what is asked *now* and the reply *now*.

We stand together at the beginning of a new understanding. How can we interpret tradition anew? How can we meaningfully and credibly present our Christian faith today to our fellow men in this world? These are the concerns of preaching and dogmatic theology.

In conclusion I should like to quote a Lutheran and then a Catholic theologian who both say the same thing from their particular angle of vision. Dietrich Bonhoeffer: "... But we too are being driven back to first principles. Atonement and redemption, regeneration, the Holy Ghost, the love of our enemies, the cross and resurrection, life in Christ and Christian discipleship—all these things have become so problematic and so remote that we hardly dare any more to speak of them.... It is not for us to prophesy the day, but the day will come when men will be called again to utter the word of God with such power as will change and renew the world" (*Letters and Papers from Prison*, London, 1953). And Karl Rahner: "The necessary and salutary reflection of the Church about itself in Vatican II will not be the final stage of theology. Another even more important one will come, for which this Council will be seen to have been simply a forerunner and indirect preparation. The ultimate truth and hope of the Church, God and his Christ, will be expressed anew as though what in fact has always been preached were really understood for the first time." ("The Teaching of Vatican II on the Church and the Future Reality of Christian Life" in *The Christian of the Future*, London, 1967).

In the common situation of starting again and exile, with its *tentatio* and *promissio*, we are united in the task of understanding anew the words and events handed down to us. Therefore the question is not primarily "What still separates us?" but "What separates us both *today* from the true Church of Jesus Christ?"

Translated by John Griffiths

John Macquarrie

What Still Separates Us
from the Catholic Church?
3. An Anglican Reply

I. The Catholic Church as a Common Heritage

WHAT still separates us from the Catholic Church? I am asked to
give an Anglican answer to this question. Needless to say, I cannot answer on behalf of all Anglicans. The Anglican communion
is noted for the great diversity of views which it embraces. Some
like to speak of the "comprehensiveness" of Anglicanism while
others would use less laudatory words and would talk of the "in-
definiteness" or even the "confusions" of Anglicanism.

Nevertheless, I think that a great many Anglicans, even an
overwhelming majority of them, will agree with me if I first of
all answer the question by saying that, in a very real and important sense, *nothing separates us from the Catholic Church*. Anglicanism has never considered itself to be a sect or denomination
originating in the sixteenth century. It continues without a break
the *Ecclesia Anglicana* founded by St Augustine thirteen centuries and more ago, though nowadays that branch of the Church
has spread far beyond the borders of England. Our present
revered leader, Arthur Michael Ramsey, is reckoned the one hun-
dredth Archbishop of Canterbury, in direct succession to Augustine himself.

It is often claimed that Anglicanism has no special doctrines
of its own and simply follows the universal teaching of the
Church. When one considers the nature of the English Reformation, one sees that there is strong support for the claim. In England there was no single dominant figure, such as Luther or

45

Calvin, who might impress upon the Church his own theological idiosyncrasies. The conscious aim of the English Reformation was to return, so far as possible, to the Catholic Christianity of the undivided Church of the first five centuries. No doubt the vision of that early Church was idealized (especially with regard to the idea that it was "undivided" and that it displayed a "uniformity", so beloved of sixteenth-century minds—and of some ecumenists today). But there was a conscious striving for continuity as well as for renewal, and the result was that the classic shape of Catholic Christianity was more clearly preserved in the English Reformation than in the more violent religious upheavals which took place in some other countries.

In spite of Puritan pressures, the Catholic tradition persisted in Anglicanism, and was powerfully reaffirmed by the Oxford Movement in the nineteenth century. In recent decades, the Catholic character of Anglicanism has been evidenced in ecumenical discussion by the insistence of Anglican theologians on the so-called Chicago-Lambeth Quadrilateral as the *minimal* characteristics of a Church fully Catholic—the Scriptures of the Old and New Testaments, the Catholic Creeds, the Dominical Sacraments and the historic Episcopate.

No doubt all Christians participate, in greater or less degree, in Catholicity. They have all maintained something of the classic form. Vatican II recognized that Anglicans had done this in a quite distinct way, and we are glad to have this recognition from our Roman brethren—it is a tremendous step forward from the old "all or nothing" position of 1896—and I shall have something to say about this later. But if we are to take this change of attitude seriously, then I must insist on changing the form of the question which stands at the head of this article. Because both Romans and Anglicans (as well as some others) have been true to the classic shape of Catholic Christianity, the question for us Anglicans is not, "What still separates us *from* the Catholic Church?" but "What still separates Anglicans and Romans *within* the Catholic Church to which they both so visibly and manifestly belong?"

In putting the question this way, I am emphasizing how much the Roman and Anglican communions have in common. They have always had much in common, but since the reforms of

Vatican II, their convergence is more apparent than ever. The celebration of the liturgy in the vernacular and the new stress on the
collegiality of the bishops are moves on the Roman side which
significantly narrow the gap with Anglicanism. There are many
minor matters where convergence has occurred, such as the pro-
posed new Roman marriage service. It is at least possible that in
the Roman communion, as in the Anglican, celibacy will come
to be regarded as a prized but optional vocation for some, and
that many parishes will be served by married priests. If present
trends continue, then the Roman and Anglican communions will
become more and more alike.

II. Serious Barriers

But although these convergences are striking, we would be de-
ceiving ourselves if we did not recognize that there are still serious
differences, and it is not likely that these will be quickly or easily
overcome. Let me mention a few of the more obvious.

(a) Let me say something first on the problem of the *Papacy*.
In the summer of 1968 I was a consultant at the Lambeth Conference, which brought together in London bishops from all over
the Anglican communion. In general, these bishops were well dis-
posed towards the Roman Catholic Church and eager for better
relations (though I wished that more of them would show as
much enthusiasm for unity with Rome as some did for rather
parochial schemes of union with Protestant bodies). But in the
midst of their deliberations, we learned of the publication of the
encyclical *Humanae vitae*. There can be no doubt that this definitely chilled the ecumenical atmosphere, so far as our relations
with Rome were concerned. Let me hasten to say that I do not
think we underestimated the difficulties confronting the Pope as
he tried to give guidance to a Church deeply divided between
progressives and conservatives. On the contrary, there was much
sympathy with him, and a recognition of his deep sincerity. But,
rightly or wrongly, it did seem to Anglican eyes that this was an
example of an autocratic action, taken without sufficient regard
to a very large and impressive body of opinion, both theological
and demographical.

This was a definite setback to the possibility of coming to some common mind on the place of the Papacy in ecumenical Christendom. Up till that point, the image of the Papacy had been steadily enhanced over a number of years. John XXIII, by his human warmth and loving spirit, had led many people outside of the Roman communion to have a new respect for the successors of St Peter. The present Holy Father also, by his concern for peace and for the poor, had gone far towards winning a place of influence and affection in the hearts of many people, both Christian and non-Christian. (His fraternal reception of the Archbishop of Canterbury had made an additional favourable impression among Anglicans.) Many Christians, including Anglicans, had begun to see in an invigorated Papacy a rallying-point for Christian action and a centre for Christian unity. But *Humanae vitae* gave a sudden check to these thoughts. It appeared once more that the Papacy concentrates in a single individual a measure of power which many Christians, including most Anglicans, find intolerable and in conflict with their understanding of the nature of the Church.

I still believe myself (and I think that many, though by no means all, Anglicans would agree) that the Papacy has an important role to play in the future of the whole Church. I do not wish to have the Papacy abolished as the price of unity, and I do not even wish to have the Pope reduced to a mere figurehead or ceremonial leader. I believe that the Papacy can provide dynamic leadership for all of us. But this can come only from a Papacy that is truly integrated with the bishops and, eventually, with the whole People of God. The Pope is a sacramental person, an embodiment of the whole Church, but he is nothing apart from the Church. Whether a renewed doctrine of the Papacy that would be acceptable to Anglicans can be worked out remains to be seen. I should think that the notion of infallibility, even in some subtly diluted form, would be quite unacceptable to most of us. So the Papacy remains at present a formidable barrier. But who knows what two hundred more years of reflection and working together may do for both Romans and Anglicans on this matter?

(*b*) The question of the Papacy, however, seems to me to be only part of a wider problem. There is in the Roman Catholic Church a *tradition of authoritarianism* with which those accustomed to less rigid structures will find it hard to come to terms.

Of course, some kind of authority is necessary in the Church if it is to retain its cohesion as the People of God and the Body of Christ. In the Anglican tradition, an attempt has been made to diffuse authority through a number of agencies, so that there is no over-concentration of authority in any single area. One of the great architects of the Anglican communion, Richard Hooker, sought a middle way between the Puritan insistence on the absolute authority of the Bible and the Roman Catholic tendency to repose authority in the Church and the hierarchy. But this middle way was no mere compromise. It was an attempt to reach a concept of authority more flexible and more responsive to the needs of the Church, and this was to be achieved by allowing the several factors constituting the authority to check and correct each other. The Bible has a certain primacy, yet it is the Bible as interpreted in the Prayer Book and under the guidance of the Church. More than this, Anglicans from Hooker to Temple have laid stress also on the authority of reason and conscience. This means in effect that Anglicans are treated as responsible adults, for whom authority is not external or oppressive.

Let me at once admit that Anglicans are not always responsible in the use of their freedom. Sometimes the Anglican communion must look, in the eyes of other Christians, like the ecclesiastical version of the "permissive society". From time to time, Anglican clergymen, theologians and even occasionally bishops, create a sensation by teaching some wildly unorthodox doctrine or by engaging in some bizarre behaviour. Anglicans have become tolerant of such eccentricities, and I do not think that many of us would wish to have it otherwise. We believe that the best answer to deviant beliefs and practices is not to try to suppress them but to bring them into the open and, by free criticism, to show what is mistaken in them as well as learning something of the truth that is hidden in every error. No doubt there is a risk in this permissiveness, but we believe that it is a risk worth taking if there is to be progress in theological understanding and in the practical application of the faith. Furthermore, it can be argued that willingness to take this risk shows a fundamental confidence in Catholic truth and in the capacity of this truth to survive in the free market of ideas. One may recall the words of St Irenaeus

about the false teachers of his day: *Adversus eos victoria est sen-
tentiae eorum manifestatio (Adv. Haer.*, I, xxxi, 4).

It is true that within recent years the concept of authority is
being subjected to renewed scrutiny in the Roman Catholic
Church, and that some of the old rigidity has been abandoned.
There is a new freedom, and it is hoped that it will be strength-
ened. But authoritarian and autocratic attitudes still persist, and
many Roman Catholic bishops still seem to have the idea that if
anyone's teaching deviates from the accepted norm, he ought to
be silenced. This would be quite unacceptable to Anglicans, and
we would need to look long and hard at any move towards closer
relations with Rome if there was any danger that this might impair the reasonable liberties which we prize.

A somewhat amusing feature of contemporary Roman Catholicism is that even supposedly "progressive" bishops still entertain
very old-fashioned ideas of authority, and try to enforce reforms
by methods quite as arbitrary and dictatorial as the "reaction-
aries" ever used in opposing reform. In the United States, we recently had the unedifying spectacle of two priests being harassed
and eventually silenced by the hierarchy, one because he was considered too progressive, the other because he still wanted a few
Latin Masses and the old ceremonial! This would have been
funny, if it had not shown to what an extent the old inflexible
ideas of authority still prevail and how much fear there is of departure from uniformity. Anglicanism could gladly accommodate
the positions of both of the priests mentioned, and if this makes
for a somewhat untidy Church, it is nevertheless one in which
there is opportunity for experiment and dialogue.

(*c*) A related question is that of *dogmatic definition*. There are,
I think, no really unbridgeable differences of doctrine between
Rome and Canterbury. Indeed, for my own part, I think that
Anglicans are much closer to Rome in their understanding of the
Christian faith than they are to Protestants—though here I must
add that, because of the wide diversities to be found within
Anglicanism, many of my brethren in the Anglican communion
would disagree with me and would believe that their affinities
were rather with Protestantism. However, Anglicans do not
attempt to formulate precise dogmatic definitions of the kind

that have multiplied in the Roman Catholic Church, and most of us would not want to be committed to such definitions.

Let me give a couple of examples of what I have in mind. Anglicans agree with Roman Catholics that the Eucharist is not merely a memorial meal but is a sacrament in which Christ is really present. This, however, is not spelled out in a precise definition in terms of transubstantiation (or transignification!) or anything of the sort, but rather it is implicit in our invariable liturgical practice (for instance, in the various Prayer Book rites and in the rubrics concerning the disposal of the consecrated Elements). There is no *one* officially received and promulgated theology of the Real Presence, though the mystery itself is unambiguously affirmed. A second example concerns the place of the Blessed Virgin Mary. Throughout the Anglican communion, her feasts are observed according to the Prayer Book. Implicit in this is a theology of her role in the economy of salvation, and an acknowledgment of the veneration which is due to her. But we do not insist that particular ways of understanding, let us say, her conception or her dormition, shall be *de fide*, as Rome has done in the dogmas of the Immaculate Conception and the Assumption.

Does this mean that Anglicanism has only a diffuse and indefinite theology? I think the answer to this question is both Yes and No. Our theology is diffuse in the sense that it is not precisely formulated; for we recognize that various formulations are possible, that these vary according to historical and cultural circumstances, and that no single formulation can claim a monopoly of truth, for it cannot be more than an approximation to truth. On the other hand, our theology is not an indefinite "Believe what you like, so long as you feel good!"; this kind of sentimentalism is just as far from Anglicanism as is rigid dogmatism, and the Prayer Book makes clear Anglican adherence to the central mysteries of the Catholic faith. It is obvious further that this flexibility in the manner of formulating belief is closely connected with the question of theological freedom, which I mentioned in the paragraphs dealing with authority.

III. IRRITANTS WHICH COULD BE OVERCOME

The problems I have talked about up till now will not be quickly solved, though I believe that there can be a gradual "growing together" and convergence of the two communions, so that these barriers will in course of time come to be less formidable. However, I think there are some minor matters that separate us from the Roman Catholic Church. These are in the nature of "irritants". It would surely not be too hard to get rid of them, and, until they are got rid of, they definitely interpose a barrier in the way of a *rapprochement* between Rome and Canterbury.

(*a*) Let me mention first the Roman Catholic attitude towards "*mixed marriages*"—marriages where one of the partners is a Roman Catholic and the other either an Anglican or an adherent of some other faith. The decree *Ne temere* requires an undertaking from the partners that all children of the marriage shall be brought up in the Roman Catholic faith. I consider this to be an oppressive requirement. I was not surprised to read recently that one branch of the Anglican communion (the Church of Ireland) has decided that its priests will no longer participate in joint marriage ceremonies with Roman Catholic priests where the *Ne temere* promise is exacted. I think this decision of the Church of Ireland is correct, for there is no true ecumenism in polite gestures against a background of ecclesiastical imperialism.

(*b*) The other irritant which divides us from genuine fellowship with our Roman brethren is the condemnation of *Anglican orders* by Rome in 1896. According to *Apostolicae curae*, Anglican orders are "utterly null and absolutely void". I know, of course, that such a harsh judgment would not (in all likelihood) be passed in the ecumenical atmosphere of today. I know also that many individual Roman Catholic theologians tell us that this judgment no longer represents the mind of the Church. I know too that Pope Paul VI made the splendid and significant gesture of giving his ring to the Archbishop of Canterbury. But in spite of all this, the condemnation remains "on the books" as the official Roman Catholic position. It is still being printed in the most recent handbooks of official Roman Catholic teaching— some of these books edited by very eminent and supposedly "progressive" theologians. What is Rome going to do about this? It will not do to say (as some Roman Catholic theologians seem to be saying) that we can sweep it under the carpet and that many of the terms of reference under which the question was discussed in 1896 no longer apply. The point is that *many of them do apply*. Perhaps a bigger question lurks in the background: can Rome never admit that it has been mistaken, or must there always be the subterfuge that one is merely "supplementing" what was said on a former occasion? What a tremendous ecumenical break-through would take place as regards Rome and Canterbury if Rome could only frankly dissociate itself from the one-sided and unjust condemnation of 1896!

My personal love and admiration for the Roman Catholic Church, and my commitment to the Catholic form of Christianity are great, and I am sorry if some things in this article may seem harsh. But the kind of ecumenism which glosses over genuine differences with ambiguous phrases and sentimental claptrap is worse than useless. So is the impatient kind that demands immediate intercommunion as if differences did not exist. We are historical beings, and we have to grow together historically, just as in the past we have grown apart historically. I rejoice that even now we are so close to each other, and look forward to our drawing still closer together in the decades ahead.

Hans Küng, Walter Kasper, Johannes Remmers

4. The Extent of Convergence

As Catholic theologians we cannot fail to be extremely grateful that our questions should have produced such critical, sympathetic and constructive answers, reflecting the diversity of Christianity: a Greek Orthodox, a Danish Lutheran and a Scottish Anglican teaching in the United States differ not only in background, education and temperament, but even more so in terms of faith and denomination. It is significant that the very way in which they question themselves reflects their own understanding of the unity and catholicity of the Church.

Despite the variety of these answers, which can as a whole be considered representative of a major part of Christianity outside the Catholic Church, they show a remarkably high degree of unanimity. Mutual grievances, aspirations and hopes are expressed with as much commitment to the individual Church as respect and friendship towards the Catholic Church. Having perceived the divergence of answers, it remains to determine their mutual foundation.

I. Successful Breakthrough to an Open Future

From all these answers it is evident that despite the refusal of certain members of various Churches to acknowledge it, relations between the Catholic Church and all other Churches have undergone a fundamental transformation as a result of conciliar and post-conciliar developments. No one disputes that the Catholic Church would in many respects remain unchanged, even where strictly demanded to change by the Gospel; of course post-conciliar development tends to give a very conflicting, even contradictory, impression, and, to some extent, the balance is still being maintained between progressive and reactionary trends. One development, however, cannot but be apparent to all other Churches: namely, the changes and movement within the Catholic Church, that formerly unchanging, rigid monolith—changes in its form of service, its teaching and theology, order and discipline, as well as in its relations with the other Christian Churches and the modern world.

All of a sudden there is room even in the Catholic Church (previously *semper eadem*) for unforeseen ecumenical developments. Fronts are openly moving, the lines of division now run through rather than between the Churches; after centuries of seeming immobility there now appears on the horizon the possibility of an open, mutual, ecumenical future unaffected by any previous theological or ecclesiastical traditions. Its realization may well be more remote for some Churches than for others, but instead of being regarded as a fictitious *fata morgana* it is at least accepted as a valid promise which should be pursued in the practical and theoretical renewal of each individual Church, as well as through sympathetic listening to and working with each other.

This possible ecumenical future will be achieved neither by the return of the other Churches to the bosom of the Roman mother-Church, nor by the Catholic Church bringing itself into alignment with the other Churches and the task of their own history and continuity. This *rapprochement* is more likely to be realized through the honest *metanoia* of all Churches throughout the world. In other words, a universal conversion of thought, word and action following the example of the Gospel in preparation for the world of tomorrow.

II. Withdrawal of Doctrinal Differences

It is significant that a member of the Orthodox Church should consider the *filioque* to be more a question of the one-sided authoritarian exercise of the Church's teaching authority than a divisive matter of faith; significant, too, that the Lutheran no longer holds the justification of the sinner through faith, his

articulus stantis et cadentis ecclesiae, in opposition to the Catholic
Church, but proceeds instead from this standpoint to examine
and evaluate the common needs and hopes of all Churches; significant, finally, that the Anglican lays such stress on Catholic
tradition and even expresses public sympathy towards the papacy.
This in no way means that problems in theology and dogma
have now ceased to exist: on the contrary, they are raised with
complete frankness by our discussion partners. But their importance has diminished. In the light of historical interpretation,
they are no longer considered insoluble, and therefore recede
further and further behind mutual anxieties and hopes.

III. DISPARITY BETWEEN ECCLESIASTICAL "SYSTEMS" AND THEOLOGY

From these considerations it will be apparent that progressive
theologians of the different Churches (not to be confused with
self-styled "fringe" theologians)—and to a certain extent also
official theological spokesmen—have already reached amicable
agreement on many points. From the Catholic point of view it
must be admitted that a great many Catholic theologians have
far more in common with numerous Orthodox, Protestant and
Anglican theologians than with their Catholic fellow theologians,
who still cling to the ways of thought of the Counter-Reformation, or even the Middle Ages. On the other hand, it is unfortunately apparent—and this is the root of a certain amount of
disillusionment with the ecumenical movement on the part of
the younger generation—that the ecclesiastical systems (i.e., administrative authorities and structures) still lag considerably behind the developments produced by progressive theologies.

It is particularly noticeable, but by no means unique, in the
Catholic Church that certain leaders who as pastors should in
fact be setting the pace, advance with grudging reluctance, constantly looking over their shoulders with reminders of the value
of tradition, together with those theologians who consider their
chief task to be the defence of teaching and practice under the
present system. This discrepancy between theology and Church
administration, for which the theologians are as much to blame

as the bishops and Church leaders, would seem to be one of the main reasons for the universal rise of the ecumenical movement.

IV. THE PAPACY AS THE CHIEF OBSTACLE TO ECUMENICAL UNITY

The papacy is the one issue which causes all our partners in discussion the greatest problems, both in dogma and practice. This we cannot afford to overlook, since it would seem to be the greatest stumbling-block in inter-denominational understanding. The Orthodox Church deplores the centralized legal system of the papacy (governing both Church discipline and the formulation of dogmas) which has evolved in particular since the Middle Ages. The Anglicans, despite their respect for Catholic tradition, criticize the authoritarian structures of the Catholic Church in both teaching and practice, over which the Pope seems to stand as protector and promoter. The Lutherans, while showing full understanding for the situation of the Catholic Church, nevertheless wonder whether the present Pope can be regarded as the representative and sole valid mouthpiece of the Catholic Church in view of the way in which his isolated, arbitrary actions run counter to any conciliar renewal—in particular, of course, his dogmatic utterances such as the "Credo" and the encyclical *Humanae vitae*, which to the outside world appeared to be openly anti-ecumenical actions.

This must be particularly depressing to Catholic theologians, since the very same critics of the papacy openly express their sympathy not only for the true realization of the papal office, but for the present Pope himself: and do not hesitate to criticize their own system. The only spark of hope stems from the fact that none of the spokesmen of the other Churches regards these difficulties as insuperable.

The above considerations, in both their negative as well as their positive aspects, offer much scope for reflection, requiring that hopes and grievances alike be considered with equal gravity. They demand a further, decisive development of the situation in the Catholic Church towards a common ecumenical future.

Translated by Sarah O'Brien-Twohig

Athenagoras Kokkinakis

Does Our Church Need a New Reformation?

1. An Orthodox Reply

MORE and more frequently members of the Orthodox Church are today being asked the question, "How far does your Church feel the need to undergo renewal and reformation?"

This question is often heard both at gatherings of Orthodox theologians and at conferences organized by the World Council of Churches. Orthodox Christians who live in the pluralistic society of the West frequently discuss ecclesiastical matters related to the probability of the renewal and reform of their Church.

I. CHURCH OF THE PAST AND CHURCH OF THE PRESENT

In view of the fact that their Church has passed through the tempestuous period of the sixteenth-century Reformation and that today it is in the process of renewal, Western theologians often question their Orthodox colleagues regarding their Church's intention to renew itself, and inquire whether they themselves recognize such a need.

From one point of view Eastern Orthodoxy stands before Western Christendom as the Church of tradition, the Church of the seven Ecumenical Councils, and the Early Fathers. In the dialogue between the Churches, Orthodoxy can say not only to the Protestant world but also to Rome, "We are your past". The Orthodox Church has not experienced the evolution which has affected all Christians of the West whether Roman or Reformed, during the past eight centuries. Orthodoxy has passed through no "Middle Ages" in the Western sense, no scholastic revolution such as medieval Europe knew in the thirteenth century, no Reformation and Counter-Reformation, but still preserves a more ancient way of thinking and praying which the West has for the most part forgotten.

Precisely because the historical background of Orthodox Christianity has been so different from that of the West, because Orthodoxy stands outside the circle of ideas within which all Western Christians have moved for the past millennium, Orthodoxy can often act as a catalyst in the Catholic-Protestant confrontation.

It would be indeed a grave mistake to imagine that Orthodoxy is simply static and conservative, looking solely to the past. Certainly Orthodoxy values its living and creative continuity with the ancient Christian world, but at the same time it is most emphatically a Church of the present, concerned to meet a wide variety of problems in the contemporary world. In Greece, for example, there is the urgent question of what form the alliance between Church and State is to assume in the second half of the twentieth century. In Russia and elsewhere behind the Iron Curtain, Orthodox face the challenge of a totalitarian atheist regime with which they must perforce establish some kind of *modus vivendi*, while yet safeguarding the full integrity of their Christian witness. And in the West, the Orthodox *diaspora* has the difficult task of discovering its true place and future mission within a pluralist society.

The Orthodox witness in the West seems to have made a deep impression on a considerable number of Christian thinkers and people. Many think of the Orthodox presence as a basic influence for the reorientation of Western Christian spirituality, as a guide to the reconstruction of the ecclesial aspects of Christian experience. They even look to some extent to the loose federation system of the independent National Orthodox Churches as a partial basis for the renewal of the administrative system of the Western Church.

Worship provides the most fruitful sphere of comparison. When East meets West in examining and applying methods of worship, the East is found to possess valuable resources for enriching the structure of Christian services. Prayers composed by Eastern saints and ritual practices formed by Eastern Christians have long been incorporated into Western prayer books. The most recent case is the addition of the Epiclesis in the Eucharistic Canons authorized by the Vatican a few months ago. This decision may put an end to arguments raised in the East as to the completeness and validity of the Western Eucharistic Service.

All these Eastern influences indicate that Christian Orthodoxy, though strongly attached to the past, is nevertheless able to move freely in the contemporary world and make its presence felt in a way which only the naïve can dismiss as useless and archaic. The faithful and careful Christian observers, however, cannot help but take notice of what Orthodoxy stands for, the beneficial reforms which may stem from it, and the role it may play in the work of healing the sixth wound inflicted in the Body of Christ by our schisms and divisions.

II. Continuity and Renewal

All the above indicates that Christian Orthodoxy has a great mission in our present world. Orthodoxy cannot be indifferent to the many pressures which are leading Christian Communions in the West—and not least the Roman Catholic Church—to embark on the path of renewal and reform. But while the Orthodox Church is in no sense opposed to the idea of renewal and reform of itself, within the Orthodox context any such reformation must be restricted to practical aspects of the Church's life. For Orthodox Christians the primary truths of the faith have been defined and proclaimed once and for all in the dogmatic decrees of the seven Ecumenical Councils. These dogmatic definitions possess for Orthodoxy an abiding and irrevocable validity. Naturally the Christian people in every generation must seek to make these definitions its own, entering into their inner spirit and significance, and for this purpose must take advantage of the characteristic insights afforded by the philosophical outlook and the cultural background of the age.

This is what the Greek Fathers did and we today must be no less adventurous than they. But the definitions as such cannot be cancelled or withdrawn. While no verbal formula can exhaust the mystery of the living God, the ecumenical definitions act for all time as a true signpost and guide for Christians in the way of salvation. They must direct our thinking as in the past.

With this Eastern Orthodox attitude in mind, Western historians usually observe that the Orthodox Church did not develop its theology, christology or ecclesiology. The special themes that the sixteenth-century Reformation introduced to the theological debate have not as yet found their place in the Orthodox synthesis.

But these new themes of the Reformation such as faith, grace, predestination, atonement, are not absent from what the patristically minded theologians of the East and the ecumenical decrees had implicitly and explicitly defined. One may add, however, what is the use of all these theological concepts if salvation is safeguarded and the purity of the faith is protected with what has been decreed? Christ did not theologize, neither did his Apostles. Their kerygmatic instructions offered and continue to offer an unshakable foundation for a living faith that inspires action and guidance to salvation. One must not forget where liberal theological speculation, detached from the sources of traditional Christian thought and piety, has led some contemporary thinkers. The strange idea that God is dead, the empty concept of religionless Christianity, are simply products of so-called progressive theological philosophizing, the development of a theology on the existential pattern. Compare this chaotic situation with the apophatic patristic theology which still guides the mind of the Orthodox Church and the exponents of its theology, and you will see why the Eastern Church emphasizes its attachment to the ecumenical definitions as signposts and guides to the true Christian faith and salvation.

But alongside these primary and unalterable truths on which our Orthodox faith is based, there are in addition many secondary questions, practical, liturgical and administrative, relating to the daily life of the Church. Here there is indeed great scope for reinterpretation, renewal and reformation.

Local reforming movements have in fact occurred several times in Orthodox history, for instance, the correction of the liturgical books by Patriarch Nicon of Moscow in the middle of the sixteenth century, the translation of the New Testament into modern Greek idiom (1896–1901), and the change of the calendar by the Greek and other Orthodox Churches in 1924. Significantly these reforms provoked conservative schisms which persist to the present time, and this indicates the grave danger of advancing too hastily, a danger of which thoughtful Roman Catholics are today acutely conscious.

III. Practical Questions

A questionnaire which cannot be quoted here at length lists a number of areas in which many contemporary Orthodox consider a renewal and reform possible and desirable. It is an unofficial questionnaire prepared on my private initiative which has been sent to various Orthodox bishops, priests and lay theologians, in an effort to make clearer the consensus of Orthodox opinion concerning the renewal of our Church life.

Many of the questions are liturgical, the possible simplification and abbreviation of our services, the provision of a new lectionary, with greater employment of the Old Testament, the recitation of the Eucharistic Canon aloud, the celebration of more than one Liturgy by the same priest in the course of a single day. In particular, the questionnaire calls attention to two obscure and debated points in the Divine Liturgy, the particles on the paten, and the difference in the Epiclesis in the two main Orthodox Eucharistic Liturgies. The rest of the questionnaire is devoted to moral, disciplinary and administrative themes, rules of fasting, the relevance of certain canons in the modern world, birth control, the possibility of married bishops, the possibility of allowing ordained deacons and priests to marry, *aggiornamento* in clerical dress and titles, the desirability of the Orthodox *diaspora* observing Easter on the Western date.

I do not suggest that these are the only questions of importance in our contemporary Church life, nor do I wish to pre-judge the answers which ought to be given. But undoubtedly these are among the many issues which the Orthodox Church of today needs to discuss, as it continues with its unceasing task of bringing men to Christ.

I must confess that in preparing this questionnaire I have asked leading questions and trodden unapproachable ground which is sacred. I submitted it, however, to Orthodox clergy and laymen with timidity and hesitation and in fear of God.

Nevertheless, the widespread recognition of the contemporary needs of the Orthodox ministry, the multiform problems faced by the Orthodox people everywhere, the widely recognized readiness for a kind of renewal of our Church expressed by many Orthodox prelates and laymen, make me feel that something good will come out of this debate, for the benefit of the people of Christ.

Hébert Roux

Does Our Church Need a New Reformation?

2. A Protestant Reply

I. Reform as a Continuing Duty

ANY Protestant answer to this question is all too likely to be just one more variation on the well-known theme of *ecclesia reformata semper reformanda*. The Churches born out of the sixteenth-century Reformation have, after all, always admitted in theory that the true Church of Christ is a Church that is ever ready to be reformed according to God's word, under the guidance of the Holy Spirit. Indeed the permanent reformation of the Church as a human institution became part of Protestant ecclesiology, bringing with it its own norms and dynamism whose "logical" development would provide a facile and reassuring answer to the question under consideration.

But there are two major reasons why we must not beg the question in any such simplistic way.

(*a*) First an historical reason: it is undeniable that within the various Protestant faiths as historically developed into national and autocephalous Churches, the weight of institutions, the rigidity of doctrine, the Church-centredness, and lastly the attachment to "traditions" dependent on entirely non-theological factors, have combined all too often to give the lie to the *semper reformanda* of our fine theorizing. One could quote numerous examples of this, even in the present-day apostolic activity of Protestantism, which has all too frequently been coupled with a movement of expansionism, or with the determination to export to other cultures certain types of confessional institution of a purely Western kind.

(*b*) Then a factual reason, connected with the historical one: the existence of ecclesiological pluralism within Protestantism. In effect, the term "our Church", as a collective singular used in the Protestant vocabulary, does not describe the same organic reality, or reality of communion, that it does for a Catholic, an Orthodox, or even an Anglican.

There is not *one* Protestant Church, but several. Even though one may recognize the relationship—even the identity—of some creeds, or some forms of ecclesiastical government, one cannot assume *a priori* that there will be a consensus among them in regard to what we may call a *new* reformation, nor even in regard to what should be held to be reformable or irreformable in the Church. The fact that the dialogue between the Catholic and Protestant Churches tends to become channelled into world-wide federations or alliances which exist quite apart from what took place in the World Council, is not merely evidence of this kind of ecclesiological pluralism, but may even contribute to accentuating it. One can no longer ignore the existence in Protestantism the world over of many living communities that are congregationalist and charismatic in form, for whom the problem of reforming the Church is seen primarily in terms of spirituality and experience, rather than of theology or institutions.

Finally, if one looks at the question from the standpoint of *needs*, one may think that these will vary with situations and places, and thus be felt and expressed very differently by, say, a Scandinavian Lutheran, a South American Methodist or a French Protestant.

However precise and realistic we try to be in answering the question, another reformation for "our Church" can only be personalized, limited and partial, even though it may actually meet with the approval of many people.

These first comments might tempt one to conclude that the most urgent objective for any new reformation must really be to bring about an actual organic unity of all the Churches we speak of as "Reformed". We are well aware that with the support of the World Council of Churches—though not by its initiative—a great many unions or reunions among Churches have recently come about; in other cases there has been failure or postponement. Without passing any judgment on such undertakings, one may none the less suggest that in most cases they have been the result of bilateral agreements, understandings reached or expressed, involving mutual recognition of the validity of existing ministerial or sacramental institutions—rather than the fruit of any genuine ecclesial reform within the parties concerned. If it is true, as our experience of the ecumenical movement would seem to show, that the quest for unity goes hand-in-hand with the demand for an authentic internal renewal of all the various Churches, then one must certainly consider what are the needs which make it essential to have a new reformation, as well as the purposes, the norms and the criteria of that reformation.

Now it is quite clear that within the Protestant Churches such inquiries are far from meeting with unanimous answers at the moment. It is true that Protestantism adapts very well to the (at times paradoxical) coexistence of an outworn conservatism with a fervent reformism. The Protestant loves "his Church" enough to be willing at times to criticize or decry it; but it remains true that, when it comes actually to promoting reforms, to analysing the situations that demand them, and working out the objectives to be aimed at, then the tensions and divisions which Père Congar describes in his article on "post-ecumenism" re-emerge and indeed become more marked than ever.

II. Two Approaches: Revolution or Restoration?

There are some who see the necessary reformation as something being forced upon the Church from outside, arising out of the demands made on it by the world. To become a Church for other people makes it stop being a Church in itself, and become re-born so that its presence to a secularized world is expressed in completely new ways, in order to help mankind in search of its own future, by giving full value to the real problems posed by the development of our culture and of the socio-political aspect of human relationships. The reformation of the Church can then take place only through a *revolution*—in other words by a more or less violent or systematic break, not merely with the institution of the Church, which has throughout history worked hand-in-glove with the forces degrading, oppressing and alienating human beings, but also with all the forms in which faith has been expressed or confessed, since by their dogmatism they have hardened and sustained divisions among different Christians, and made the pure Gospel message of love and justice either incomprehensible or irrelevant to modern man.

But there are others who see the Church as bearing within itself its own force for inner renewal. All that is then needed is to rediscover its specific essence and dynamism. In establishing the twofold principle of the authority of Scripture, and justification by faith alone, the sixteenth-century Reformers showed the basis and meaning of all true reform. What we have to do is to get back to that, to discover its relevance now in terms of what the word of God is saying to the Church, the key to the mystery of man's life, and his salvation through grace from amid a sinful world. Any new reformation, therefore, can only be a *restoration*, within a closed system of doctrinal truths and ethical values that represent the "heritage" of the Reformation which must be safeguarded; and to safeguard this involves the preservation of our confession of faith, and a careful handling of the traditional structures of the Church—actions which will in themselves provide a sufficient and necessary guarantee of continuity. Ultimately this must lead either to the visible Church's destroying itself or being dissolved or broken into a series of one-dimensional evangelisms, or to a complacent self-justification on the part of the different ecclesial forms of an ever more irredentist Protestantism. These two tendencies correspond to the double temptation which Karl Barth warned against thirty years ago: the "flight into invisibility" and the "flight into visibility". They are two opposite ways of turning one's back on the original vocation of the Reformation.

III. The Gospel as an Instrument of Criticism

These two tendencies, to revolution or restoration, cannot, if pushed to their limits, be reconciled. There is no possibility of finding any *via media* between them. But to the extent that both claim fidelity to the Gospel of Christ, theology's chief task should be to discover through close criticism just what is good in each of them. Now this task, which is needed in any reformation, demands at least two conditions:

(*a*) We must clarify, if not clearly elucidate, the complex of problems relating to Scripture as the *locus* of Revelation and of our hearing of the Word of God, interpreting it, handing it on, and carrying it out in the life of faith as our response and our witness to the Gospel. This implies that, in Protestant theology, we must get beyond the debates that keep arising between fideism and fundamentalism, the subjectivity and objectivity of faith, and reach a certain consensus on just what we mean by *biblical* theology and its ecclesiological and ethical implications.

(*b*) There is a need to recognize—as indeed we have begun to do—and genuinely to respect the *ecumenical* dimension of all theological research, both in space and in time. In other words, such research cannot be carried out simply in terms of "dialogue" between Churches which are all faced with the same calls for help, the same doubts, the same urgent needs of the present-day world, but must also contribute in more than merely a verbal or theoretical way towards helping the Protestant Churches in particular to understand what they are saying and doing when they say they "confess the Christian faith in communion with the Universal Church". No "new" reformation is conceivable in the Reformed Churches without this kind of awareness of the communal "Catholicity" of the Church. It should, most especially, enable us to shake off our anti-Catholic reflexes, by giving us a deeper and more precise understanding of the meaning of tradition, of apostolic succession, and of the relationship between the local and the universal Church.

But these two conditions lead us to a third which may in fact be the major condition for any authentic reformation. It consists in *recognizing the true identity of the one and only "Reformer" of the Church*. Otherwise we shall always be left with a series of reforms which, though they may be opportune and useful, are ultimately the work of the Church working upon, and for the sake of, itself alone. Even if there could be a pan-Christian Council with the objective of uniting all the Churches in one great movement of reformation, it could only be achieved by *Christ himself*. To say this is not to blur the problem by taking refuge in the sphere of pure spirituality and praying in passive expectation of a miracle. It means recognizing the concrete reality involved in the teaching and preaching—in both Old and New

Testaments—of the *metanoia*. Obviously the Churches do not underestimate the importance of repentance, conversion or penance as themes for preaching, nor their value as means to personal sanctification.

It may even be thought that Protestantism for its part—though it is not alone in this—has contributed greatly to the development of this biblical notion along individualist, pietistic and moralizing lines. But what we are really concerned with here are the specifically *ecclesiological* implications of *metanoia*, its application to the Church as such. If unity in the one faith is a *sine qua non* for Church unity, why should we reject a similar demand for unanimity in repentance? Surely the call to one is always inseparably linked with the call to the other. "Repent and believe." It was the response to that twofold call that created the Church at Pentecost, the "new Israel", the People of the New Covenant who were henceforth looking forward to the future historic and eschatological coming of the Lord. The objection so often made that repentance concerns individual members of the Church, rather than the Church itself as a divine and holy institution, cannot be sustained; for, first of all, repentance is the sign of true holiness, and secondly, the institutions of the Church are always embodied in, and made to function by, individuals. Thus it is precisely to the extent that the Church "repents"—in other words, ceases to turn in upon itself, talking to itself, justifying itself, and generally being complacent—in order to "turn outwards", to "be converted" to its Lord, that reformation becomes a possibility. "For the Lord has created a new thing on the earth", we read in Jeremiah (31. 22), "a woman shall seek her husband." The mystery of the Church is inseparable from the mystery of Christ. But it is a mystery that remains incommunicable if it is not expressed visibly in the behaviour of the Church.

At the level of the *teaching function*, any application of a strict Christo-centrism must respect the distinction between "the mystery of faith" which is Christ, and the dogmatic formulations of our "confession of faith", which, though an absolutely necessary response on our part, will always be partial, relative and provisional.

At the level of the *governing function*, especially in the

Protestant Churches, it is a question of finding once more our sense of order in liberty, not in the juridical sense, but in the theological and pastoral sense, "marching orders" which must be received and followed together (in synodal form!), presupposing what Harvey Cox calls the proper use of power.

Finally, at the level of the *prophetic function* of the Christian people in the world, that same Christo-centrism demands that we see in their true proportion the various demands relating to our necessary commitments in life and activity "in the world", with the help of a resolutely christological ethics and understanding of humanity, which will make it possible at last to see beyond the sterile oppositions we now establish between institution and event, dogmatism and prophecy, the Church in itself and the Church for the world. For truly, no house divided against itself can stand.

If the Church were to cease to be "built into ... a dwelling place of *God* in the Spirit" (Eph. 2. 22), how could it survive except as an historical ruin deserted also by *men*?

Translated by Rosemary Middleton

Stephen Neill

Does Our Church need a New Reformation?
3. An Anglican Reply

THE wisest man in the world would find it hard to give *the* Anglican answer to any question. It is not easy for those who are not Anglicans to remember all the time that the Anglican Communion is a loose federation of fifteen entirely independent Churches in all parts of the world, with a number of non-provincial dioceses, held together by a common liturgical tradition, an intense but hardly definable loyalty, a central Executive with a minute staff, and by attendance at the Lambeth Conference of bishops, summoned fairly regularly but unofficially by the Archbishop of Canterbury.

Even so, it is hard to draw a hard and fast line between what is and what is not Anglican. Most Anglican Churches have full inter-communion with the Old Catholic Churches in Europe and America, and with the small Episcopal Churches in Spain and Portugal, limited communion with the Churches of Finland and Sweden, and with the Mar Thoma (Reformed) Syrian Church of South India, the Independent Church of the Philippines and the Church of South India. Anglican Churches are engaged in re-union negotiations in Canada and the United States, Great Britain, East and West and Central Africa, North India and New Zealand. If these negotiations are successful, some Anglican Churches will disappear in united Churches into which it is held that the whole Anglican substance has been incorporated without loss.

This is as it should be. The Anglican Churches have never

claimed for themselves either universality or eternity. Most Anglicans, like most adherents of other Christian fellowships, in their heart of hearts think that if only all other Christians could be sensible and adopt a moderate Anglican position, all problems of Christian unity would be solved. But their continuing sense of the unity of the whole Christian fellowship in heaven and on earth makes it easy for Anglicans to think of a time, perhaps a distant time, at which all Anglican values will have been so safeguarded in wider fellowships that a separate Anglican existence is no longer necessary. This view was quite clearly stated by the Lambeth Conference of 1948.

The Church of England is the oldest and largest Church in the Anglican fellowship; but circumstances of history have tied it more closely than other Churches to the sixteenth century, and for this reason it is today almost the least typically Anglican among all the Anglican Churches. Yet, because of its size and antiquity, it is almost inevitable that a writer should take it, even today, as his starting-point, and note the divergences as they appear in the more independent bodies.

Few Anglicans are likely to question the basic principles of that essentially conservative movement, the Anglican Reformation of the sixteenth century. These may be briefly defined as follows:

> The supremacy of Holy Scripture as the sole authority for the faith and life of the Church. Traditions, however venerable, do not constitute a second authority; they are always commentary on the text, which is to be found only in the canonical Scriptures of the Old and New Testaments.
>
> Ancient rites, ceremonies and customs, even doctrines, need not be changed, unless they are seen to be clearly contradictory to what is to be found in Holy Scripture.
>
> All worship is to be in a language understood by the people, and the reading and exposition of Scripture is to play a large part in it.
>
> The Bible is to be in the hands of all the faithful who are to be encouraged to read it for themselves.

But history has not stood still; the principles need to be set forth in new ways that are relevant to the circumstances of the twentieth century.

I. Relationship between State and Church

The Reformation left the Church of England closely tied to the Crown. Queen Elizabeth I declared herself to be the supreme governor of the Church of England. She never abandoned the noble ideal of one people, called under one aspect the commonalty and under another the spiritualty, living in the fear of God under one divinely appointed ruler, whose task it was under God to care for their well-being under both aspects of their life. By the end of the Queen's reign this ideal was already an anachronism. The obduracy of recusants (Roman Catholics) and sectaries (dissenters) had made it clear that not all the Queen's subjects could be brought to live together in one single Church, however excellent. But the Church of England continued to be the Church of the sovereign and of the great majority of the English people. Royal control has been, if anything, less burdensome than that exercised up till 1918 in Austria by the Emperor, and in France until 1905 by ministers of the interior, a number of whom were not in any sense Christians. The link between Church and State is expressed by the presence in the House of Lords of twenty-one bishops, and the consequent exclusion from the House of Commons of Anglican clergy, who are thus constituted the least privileged of all the adult subjects of the Crown. Appointments to all diocesan bishoprics are made by the Crown on the advice of the prime minister. This system works reasonably well in practice, but is unfortunately accompanied by a horrifying and farcical election by the Dean and Chapter, who know perfectly well that no Dean and Chapter in 437 years have ever rejected the royal nominee.

Obviously it is desirable on all grounds that this system should be changed. What is desirable has been made necessary by progress towards Christian unity. No Free Church in England could honestly enter into unity with the Church of England, as long as the existing system is maintained. There is much less hostility to the idea of an established Church than there was a century ago. Even the Free Churches see that it is to the advantage of all that great national events such as the coronation of a queen are accompanied by a solemn religious ceremony. But they would demand far greater spiritual freedom for a Church which is still in many respects under parliamentary control. Unfortunately Anglican efforts in this direction have been marred by extreme timidity. Whereas the (Presbyterian) Church in Scotland long ago obtained recognition of its position as the national Church of Scotland, with at the same time the most scrupulous safeguarding of the crown rights of Jesus Christ as the only ruler of his Church, the Church of England, which could probably obtain without great difficulty similar recognition, halts and stumbles on the brink.

This is a problem that does not exist in any other part of the Anglican Communion, where the bonds of unity between Church and State, if they ever existed, have long ago been loosed. It appears that the only country in which Anglican clergy are paid by the State is Belgium.

II. Renewal of Liturgical Worship

Far more influence is exercised on the minds of the members of a Church by its forms of liturgical worship than by its formal statements of doctrine. The first complete Anglican liturgy appeared in 1549, a noble document containing some of the finest prose in the English language. But this first effort was not regarded as perfect; it was revised in 1552, 1559, 1604 and 1662, while a markedly different liturgy was provided for Scotland in 1637. After that date the liturgy became frozen by the Act of Uniformity of 1662. Liturgy never stands still. A certain number of modifications were permitted by statute. Custom produced a great many more variations. But it was felt by many that, in spite of the superlative quality of the liturgical work of the sixteenth century, worship has been drifting further and further away from the needs of the ordinary worshipper, and that far more drastic attention needed to be paid to the whole question of liturgical revision.

The Anglican Churches outside England have exercised their freedom to revise their Prayer Books. On the whole, however, these efforts have retained the traditional structures with more or less extensive modifications. In a number of cases (the United States, India), Cranmer's already somewhat prolix liturgies have become even more prolix through the effort to get into them everything that could possibly be packed in. Only in quite recent times has more radical thought been directed to the questions, What is worship? and How can Christian worship find the right and appropriate vehicles in the twentieth century? War is far too serious a business to be entrusted to soldiers. Those who survey recent Anglican experiments in the production of new liturgies may be inclined to remark that liturgical work is far too serious a matter to be entrusted to liturgiologists. Many of them seem to have worked under the illusion that liturgical changes can be made without a corresponding change in the theology to which expression is being given. This is not so. Every liturgical change does imply, even if it does not express, a modification in theology. Before a new liturgy can have any hope of lasting success, it is essential that both the makers of liturgies and those who use them should have a clear understanding of the theological purpose that underlies the work.

The present time is not favourable in England, or in the English-speaking world, for this kind of work. We are not agreed as to what can be taken for dignified, but contemporary, English. Nor are we agreed as to the theology to which we wish to give expression in liturgical form. Our contemporary revisers seem to have made Cranmer's principle stand on its head. He believed that the Church must be given the very best in liturgical form and that the worshippers must be educated up to appreciation of the treasure that had been given them, an aim which was to a surprising extent achieved in the days in which everyone willy-nilly went to church. Today it seems that we are agreed that liturgy must be brought down to the level of what the ordinary church-goer can take; our new liturgies tend therefore to reflect the spiritual impoverishment of the twentieth century over against the splendid wealth of the sixteenth.

III. Church in a Changed Modern World

In the sixteenth century, England, like India today, was a land of villages. It was the aim of the Church to place in every village an educated gentleman; the Anglican village church is a treasure greater even than the splendid cathedrals, among which one of the greatest, St Paul's in London, was built after the Reformation. Today England is a land of cities. The Church here, as in every other industrialized country in the world, has suffered by the change. There seems something in the climate of the city that makes it difficult for the ordinary man to take seriously any obligation as a worshipping member of a Church. Roman Catholic statistics in Britain and elsewhere show the leakage from which that Church like every other suffers in the industrial areas.

Yet, although de-christianization has gone very far, it is also far from being complete. There is an immense amount of diffused Christianity still present among all classes in the country. Not more than ten per cent of the population declares itself to be without any religious faith at all. Criticisms of the Church are aplenty; but in all opinion polls the great majority of those who answer state that they would rather have the Church there than see it disappear. Ignorance of Church doctrine is profound. Many have been to some extent affected by the virulent anti-Christian propaganda which has been carried on in England for more than a century. But for the person of Jesus Christ there is deep reverence, not always accompanied by any deep understanding of the principles for which he stood. In the period between 1900 and 1930 a number of intellectuals were actuated by a personal and venomous hatred of Jesus Christ, as is made undisguisedly clear in Michael Holroyd's recent biography of Lytton Strachey; this seems hardly to have registered in the consciousness of ordinary people, who still hold that, if everyone lived according to the principles laid down by Jesus Christ, the world would be a very much better place than it is.

The problem is to find ways by which this diffused but not ungenerous faith can be brought back into relationship with the Church and with the life of worship. Some would be inclined to despair completely of the organized Church, of parishes and institutions and a paid ministry and all the paraphernalia of Church administration. Others would not go so far, and, while recognizing the need for extensive modification and experiment, still hold that there is value in structures.

With the rural parishes much can be done. In these days of almost universal motor transport, the old ideal of one educated gentleman in each village can be replaced by the more flexible concept of a group of educated priests serving together a considerable number of villages. Something, no doubt, is lost; but only in some such manner will it be possible to serve the villages at all. The city presents far greater problems. Here, both in Britain and elsewhere, a number of radical experiments have been tried—the house church, in which the Lord's Supper is brought directly into the place where people live; special ministries of counselling and pastoral care; city churches which have live work on week-days and hardly exist on Sundays when the streets are almost deserted and peace reigns. It cannot be said that perfect answers have as yet been found to any problems; but those who are prepared to experiment know that out of ten experiments seven will almost certainly have to be written off as failures, but that it is worth making the ten for the sake of the three that may survive.

IV. Need for a De-clericalization

It is clear at every point that the lay people must be brought back into the centre of the life and witness of the Church. The English Reformation was largely a laymen's reformation; but ere long the Church had become thoroughly clericalized, and has never quite managed to throw off the yoke.

The Church of England is in the worst case of all, having not yet obtained the liberation brought by synodical government. This has existed for more than a century in some other provinces. The Church of Ireland, for its Representative Body, has the sound rule that there must be two laymen for every clergyman. Most of the provinces, though not all, admit women on the same basis as men. In England the change will at last take place in 1970, when a true synod will come into existence. Even in 1969 the final debate on the plans for union with the Methodists had to take place in the Convocations of Canterbury and York, purely clerical assemblies in which the "establishment" of deans, provosts and archdeacons was far too heavily represented. Even when the lay-men do come into their own, care will have to be taken to see that the Synod meets at such times and places as will make it possible for lay members to attend without too much disruption of their ordinary life; little is gained if the laymen who attend are "clericalized" laymen, out of touch with the realities of life in a fiercely competitive world.

The laymen's movement is one of the great ecumenical realities of the modern world. But those who are most eager to see the lay-folk take their full place in the witness of the Church to the world become increasingly aghast as they become aware of the spiritual illiteracy in which most lay people live, and of their total incapacity to meet the Marxist, the humanist, the secularist, on their own ground, and to give a good account of themselves as Christians. It is good that the clergy should learn to keep in the background; but they can do so only if the laity are prepared to put themselves to school, and to accept as their share of the new reformation the enormous process of re-education for which the Church must provide and to which the lay people must be prepared to submit. This can come about only as each parish becomes what it ought to be—the layman's university.

There has been much discussion in recent years as to the aims and nature of training for the ordained ministry. Perhaps the most lasting fruit of the Reformations, the Tridentine included, was a new sense of the need for professional training for the clergy. The Anglican Churches have done little in this direction compared with other bodies. In the English-speaking dominions the standard of clerical learning is admitted to be deplorably low. In the United States things are better. But in Africa, for instance, the Anglican Churches have as yet made hardly any provision for an African graduate in arts or science to study theology in his own country. In England the situation is chaotic; it is possible for a student in the Church of England to pass the General Ordination Examination and to be ordained without having read a single serious theological work—a good pass in the examination can be obtained by the use of lecture notes, and by a devout attention to little manuals. Priests trained on this kind of level cannot possibly hope to hold their own in a world in which general standards of education are daily rising.

Much stress is laid on the training of the would-be priest in the practical disciplines, religious sociology and the rest. It may be thought that this is putting the cart before the horse—that training in such fields needs to be provided for the man who has already been ordained, and that in his period of pre-ordination study what he needs to learn is how to ponder on a far deeper level than is generally the case today the mystery of godliness seen in flesh and the basic doctrines which the Church exists to teach.

V. New Pentecostal Enthusiasm

For, when all is said and done, the only reformation that in the end matters is theological reformation—a rediscovery of divine truth such as causes men and women to see visions and to dream dreams, to commit themselves with the hilarity of great adventure to the cause of Christ, and to set themselves anew to the task of bringing every thought into captivity to the mind of Christ. The Anglican Churches have a great tradition in theology. Today there is no lack of thinkers, who are making "soundings" all over the place. If they have struck oil, it seems that up to date it is no more than a rather feeble trickle. But, in the spiritual realm no less than in the physical, it often happens that soundings have to be carried out for a long time before the real treasure is discovered. We have no right to be impatient.

In the sixteenth century the Anglican Reformation was firmly grounded by its fathers on the doctrine of Justification by Faith, as "a most wholesome doctrine, and very full of comfort" (art. XI). The Puritans, by no means all of whom left the national Church, added emphasis on personal conversion to faith in Christ. The Cambridge Platonists and the Caroline divines pleaded the cause of learning and right reason in theology. John Wesley proclaimed "practical holiness" throughout the land. The Evangelicals in the Church of England fought the battle of social righteousness and missionary endeavour. The Tractarians stressed the beauty of holiness in worship and in life. The Christian Socialists looked for the transformation of the whole life of society under the power of the Gospel. The liberals won back for us a knowledge of the humanity of the Redeemer. The Student Christian Movement prepared the way for recognition of the international and ecumenical dimensions of the Gospel. What is there left for anyone to do today?

The answer may be that we have never yet taken seriously the doctrine of the Holy Spirit. Here and there in the Anglican world there have been manifestations of a new Pentecostal enthusiasm, very disturbing to right-minded people like bishops. These may be no more than ejaculations of hot air. But those who remember the way in which every movement has been criticized, reviled and rejected may be inclined to suspend judgment, recognizing at least the possibility that these Anglicans, in perhaps eccentric ways, are pointing the way to the new Reformation that could set the whole Church ablaze even in the rather unpromising circumstances of the last third of the twentieth century.

Johannes Baptist Metz

Does Our Church Need a
New Reformation?
4. A Catholic Reply

MY specialism is not ecumenical studies. Anyway, to make ecumenism a special branch of theology is hardly an adequate solution. Ultimately, ecumenism is not a local but a universal and radical theological commitment. The unity of Christians today cannot come merely from the good will and theological efforts of the few; it is demanded of all, and all must make it their concern. Nowadays we have to speak and act ecumenically without any special commission.

I should like to submit two theses on the situation peculiar to ecumenism at the present moment. The first is concerned with the intrinsic connection between ecumenism and ecclesiastical reform, and is also an attempt to answer the question "Does the Church need a new Reformation?" The second has to do with the phenomenon of indirect ecumenism—with the way in which Christian unity is effected through the problems of world unity, and hence with the so-called "post-ecumenical era" so often postulated today.

I

First thesis: Nowadays any really effective progress in Christian unity is inseparably bound up with change in the structures and public activity of the Churches themselves. Internally, the ecumenical question has become a question of ecclesiastical reform. Therefore ecumenical activity is above all charismatic and critical work directed towards the reformation of and reform in a particular Church.

1. The intrinsic connection between ecumenism and ecclesiastical reform emphasized in this thesis is not the product of mere resignation, and scepticism about the possibilities of theological agreement. It does not mean that I advocate an anti-theological ideology of *praxis*, or a fetishism of action and change that would cancel the question of what should determine such a course of action. It is grounded wholly *in the* operational and social nature of the theological question of and search for universal truth and unity. This question can no longer be posited and answered in purely theoretical terms; it is a problem of theory *and* practice, and the open arena is the indispensable medium of the theological quest for truth and unity. This general theological consideration cannot be pursued further here.

We must take for granted that all theological progress in unity requires not only historical but social verification in public and in the transformed practice of the Church itself. This is the only way in which the process of ecumenism can be freed from abstraction, and thus from transience, irresolution and concrete untruth.

Of course, in addition to this general theological consideration there is a specific connection between ecumenism and ecclesiastical reform. I should like to draw attention to two aspects of this specific context.

Firstly, nowadays we have to assume that it is no longer possible to present and determine unity and difference of belief in a "purely theological" context. The reason for this is, I think, to be found in the growing internal pluralism of theologies themselves. This pluralism is irrevocable, and affects not only secondary theological problems but the interpretation of the whole reality of faith.

It is surely true to say that the frontiers of modern theology run right across confessional boundaries. In this case, how could theology itself determine and guarantee the distinctive unity of what it is concerned with? The quest for unity of faith is of itself transformed into a practical quest. Its dwelling-place is not pure theology but that body of principles which is the Churches' profession of faith in practice. But doesn't this mean that every effective demand for unity of the Churches is called in question? Isn't every quest for unity positivistically and decisively to be referred to the current practice of the Church? Among the conditions for an advance in ecumenism that are put forward only one seems to me really possible: an actual transformation of the practical life of the Churches and of the structures within which it is lived. Only on the long road of such reforms will a change also be brought about in the mentalities which separate us implicitly and which no form of theological reflection can possibly assimilate to one another. This consideration reveals the relation between ecumenism and ecclesiastical reform that I have posited. As an exemplar of critical freedom in the Church, theology can and must become a locus of initiative for change, and of emancipation from certain determined activities and structures of the Church.

Secondly, the problem of ecumenism includes the *dimension of history*—or the dimension of unity defrauded of realization in history as it has been lived. The connection of the problem of unity with the problem of history means that unity cannot be obtained merely by inquiry and speculation. History is the experience of reality in conflicts that cannot be expiated and reconciled by the manipulation of concepts alone. They are conflicts that can be resolved only in practice. Christendom's historical forfeiture of identity cannot be cancelled simply by offering a novel interpretation of Christian traditions. A purely conceptual attitude to the history of division would itself remain a victim of the untruth into which our actions in history have caused us to fall. Accordingly, we shall be able to preserve the evangelical tradition and promise of unity only if we help in the task of renewing contemporary conditions, practice and modes of life in the Churches. Ecumenical theology will be able to avoid a noncommittal mystification of the notion of unity in Christ, an ideological misapplication of it to obscure the actual divisions between Christians, only if it faces up to and transforms the present conditions of ecclesiastical and Christian life itself, in which the unity sought and longed for cannot be found.

2. As far as the Catholic Church is concerned (and that is the Communion with which I am expressly concerned here), this ecclesiastical reform and renewal of the practice and structures of the Church began with the Vatican Council. And so the Council was—in a very meaningful sense—"ecumenical", inasmuch as

it was or tried to be a Council for the renewal of the Church. Of course it is also true that a crisis in the renewal that commenced with the Council must become a crisis (perhaps, indeed, the decisive one) of contemporary ecumenism itself.

It doesn't mean that I am a victim of the universally prevalent crisis jargon, if I refer to the contemporary Church in terms of a crisis of renewal and claim to discern in it symptoms of a "modern Counter-Reformation"—a movement against the Council for reform of the Church. I don't mean primarily in terms of content, but formally and fundamentally: as resistance to the "spirit of the Council", as a counter-reformation that at times, in authoritarian measures "from above" and expectations "from below" of authoritarian decisions, would seem to fear nothing more than the "authority of freedom" itself—which was proclaimed so impressively at the Council. A number of such "counter-reformatory" symptoms have announced themselves: the seemingly almost constitutional mistrust of the charismatic freedom of the Spirit, the often merely simulated appearances of maturity; the attempts religiously and spiritually to cast suspicion on the decisive spirit of reform and to disown it as liberal minimalism; the lack of continued heart among us theologians ourselves—of courage to answer for the ecclesiastical and social consequences of theological renewal. But I haven't space here for a full discussion of these symptoms, which I have tried to outline in a short book.[1]

3. I should like to mention at least one of the elements of ecclesiastical reform which were established in the Council, and which could be decisively important for the advance of ecumenism if verified by adoption in the transformed practical life of the Church. After the significance that the fundamental definition of the Church as the "people of God" can have for the understanding of the offices of the Church and their practice; after the significance that the proclamation of religious freedom can acquire for the understanding of ecclesiastical religion and its

---

[1] J. B. Metz, *Reform und Gegenreformation heute. Zwei Thesen zur ökumenischen Situation der Kirchen* (Mainz and Munich, 1969). The two theses I put forward in this article form a considerably shortened version of the argument of this book on reform and counter-reformation today.

structures, and a religion of freedom,[2] I wish to refer summarily
to the following element of ecclesiastical reform: The eschatological distinction between the institutional Church and the kingdom
of God (for the sake of which it exists) is clearly expressed in the
conciliar understanding of the Church.

It is seen to be obvious that the Church is not here for its own
sake; that it understands itself rather as "God's eschatological
provisional arrangement"; and that therefore it lives also by the
proclamation of its own eschatological transience. When this
eschatological distinction between Church and kingdom is effective in the self-understanding and life of the Church, it is possible
for a new, positive relationship to form within the Church towards those Christians who identify themselves only in part with
the existing institution. This seems to me of great importance,
not least of all for the reform movement in the Church and
especially for the ecumenical question. At present there are many
—very many—Christians who are only partly "identified" in an
institutional sense. If they are to be taken seriously and not
simply left on the periphery, they force us—in their own
specific terms—to recognize the distinction between Christendom
and the Church, and prevent us from taking the question of the
"Church" only to the limits of the institution itself. We are not
concerned simply with Christians outside any Church; those I am
referring to feel only too surely that a wholly non-institutional
Christianity would, in our a-historical society, also lose touch
with Christian tradition itself. Nevertheless, in theology and in
the Church we have no criteria that are appropriate to them.
Theories of Church membership do not or only negatively correspond to this pattern of partial identification. More usually,
these Christians are characterized by negative terms, such as
"peripheral Christians" or "quasi-Christians". In this way, the
positive element that can occur in this kind of partial identification is overlooked from the start, and uncritical, more or less un-
problematical, total identification is asserted as an irrefragable
ideal.

But a Church that knows that it does not exist for its own sake,
that remains distinct from the kingdom of God to which it bears

[2] Cf. the book mentioned in note 1.

witness, and at the same time acknowledges that it is always sinfully in arrears with its proper testimony, would have to react to this partial identification as an extremely serious question. Isn't it possible for this form of Christian existence also to derive from the eschatological conscience of the believer—the critical mark of the surplus eschatological truth of Christianity that cannot find adequate room for expression in an ecclesiastical institution?

Seen in this way, this very pattern of partial identification can become a spur to reform—to changes in the form and behaviour of the Church itself. The history of heresy within Christianity is full of such patterns of partial identification. We must not forget that this chronicle of heresy was often the pre-history of ecclesiastical Christianity. Whereas in earlier times the mode of existence that we now call "partial identification" occurred only in individual cases and in small movements, it has now become a public problem for the whole Church, and one that cannot be referred to the future for resolution.

If the Church were widely to acknowledge that this partial identification *can* contain something in itself irrefutably positive that cannot simply be replaced by total identification with the institution, then an important aspect of and impulse for ecclesiastical reform would be apparent. And within the Church itself a mental framework would have been provided for a positive understanding of the particular nature of non-Catholic Christianity —spade-work for a pluralization of ecclesiality with Christianity itself.

II

Second thesis: Increasingly the drive towards ecumenism must take the form of "indirect ecumenism". The advance of theological agreement and of Christian unity will not be aided solely and primarily by direct dialogue between the Churches, but by the individual confrontation of each of the Christian Churches and their specific traditions with a "third partner"—that is, with the problems and requirements of the world today. This image of "indirect ecumenism" includes both a specific determination of the theological location of the Christian unity that is sought after, and a specific interpretative model for the formulation of Christian faith.

More than ever before, questions of Christian unity touch on world ecumenism. Not division between Christians but the divisiveness of the world in itself strikes one as the primary demand now made by the evangelical message of the unity and reconciliation of all men in Jesus Christ. In relation to traditional ecumenism, one might be tempted to see this as a "post-ecumenical" situation. But etymologically as well as in biblical usage, and in the most recent pronouncements of the ecumenical movement itself, reference is made to this dimension of ecumenicity. And the use of the term "post-ecumenical" could have a dangerous effect—could seem a sort of dispensation for those who in many respects are pre- or anti-ecumenical. It could also easily produce the misconception that the Churches ought to overcome their differences by dedicating themselves without conflict to the world, or by allowing them to disappear in the accomplishment of "purely secular" tasks. But the thesis of "indirect ecumenism" offered here is concerned to incorporate the universal problem anew in the problem of identity of Christianity and the Church, and to make it of moment for the theological and dogmatic quest for the resolution of the essential differences of Christian faith itself.

1. The Church is the Church of the Son of God, of Jesus Christ. But do we take the significance of this for our main theme seriously enough? Isn't it characteristic of this Church that it has no intrinsic identity, and that it cannot live simply by virtue of itself and the mere reproduction of its own traditions? Its foundation was the crumbling of the wall of division between Jews and heathen, the tearing of the veil of the Temple, and the transformation of the Synagogue into the Church in the midst of mankind, and for mankind. The movement into alien territory was obligatory. Therefore the Church surpasses itself by moving into that alien world to which it must always relate because it is the Church of the Son who reclaimed this "alien" country as his "own", and sealed this claim with his death for all men— even for unbelievers. This self-transcendence is not a subsequent addition to the Church but the basis of its establishment and of its distinction from the Synagogue in the classic sense. Therefore the Council's separation of the Constitution on the Church and

the Pastoral Constitution "On the Church in the World Today" seems highly dubious.

It now seems possible to offer the following formulation: *The theological location (locus theologicus) of the Christian unity lost and sought for is primarily that "alien world" which the Son reclaimed as his "own", and into which the Church must enter ever and again if it is not to lose or betray itself.* This alien territory is the place where Christians can once again find and recognize themselves in loyalty to that one commission in the face of which Christian confessionalism seems just as dubious and dangerous as nationalism in the face of one world, and racism in the face of one humanity. Therefore the *rapprochement* and unity of Christians occur, so to speak, "indirectly" and "incidentally": they come nearer to one another inasmuch as ever and again they take the risk of this emerging from their own ecclesiastical traditions, and attempt this self-transcendence in testimony to and in the service of love.

2. I shall now attempt to show what theological significance this indirect process has for the desired unity of faith, with reference to the central problem of different formulations of belief within Christianity itself. Controversial theology and ecumenical theology have shown us that there are always limits to agreement. These boundaries are not surmounted by a direct process—by a direct theological comparison of the individual professions of faith and their historical backgrounds. But how can an *indirect* process contribute to success? It starts not by confronting the individual formulations and traditions directly, but by their unification in the course of confrontation with the world and the society in which they must announce and bear witness to belief in Christ.

In the present-day theology of all confessions, various attempts are made to define Christian belief with reference to the contemporary world. These definitions seem to me to have one thing more or less in common: they interpret faith above all as an act of faith—as *fides qua creditur* (as far as possible devoid of content), as a form of man's free, non-objective decision. Whenever Christian belief is interpreted in this formalistic way, it can more or less dispense with any consideration of confessional differences, which have to do with the contents of faith. But, precisely for this reason, such an interpretation of Christian belief does very little to resolve existing confessional and dogmatic differences; it also seems to me to incur the danger of obscuring the socially critical force of Christian faith (which arises precisely from its contents and convictions), and of reducing it to a symbolic paraphrase of the modern consciousness without in any way helping to change it.

I should therefore like to consider the Christian understanding of faith with reference to our contemporary world and society from the viewpoint of content or, so to speak, of dogma. I interpret this faith in the form of *memoria*; I see Christian and dogmatic formulations of belief as formulations of *memoria*, or remembrance. By this, I don't mean the everyday kind of relating through memory to the past—the kind by which we tend to transfigure everything that has already happened. And I'm not referring to Augustinian *memoria*, but rather to that form of remembrance that presses on and calls in question our present world by reminding us of the future that has yet to be endured.

This kind of remembrance breaks through the magic circle of the dominant consciousness to redeem repressed conflicts and unsatisfied hopes; it maintains experiences of the past in opposition to the existing point of view and thereby ensures that the present understands itself. If Christian belief is understood and interpreted as this kind of memory, I think a twofold insight is obtained: First of all, it becomes clear how it is that in each case this belief can be dogmatic—a faith bound to content and confession, *fides quae creditur*; and how it is that, precisely in that way, it can realize the form of socially critical freedom which is directed towards the world and which the Christian is called to in the light of the Gospel. Secondly, it becomes evident that the traditional dogmatic and confessional formulations to which faith is bound can be understood as an actualization of this *memoria* and of its "revolutionary" power and effectiveness in criticizing the contemporary world. Hence they are formulations in which the claims of past promises and past hopes—once experienced and acquired—are again called to mind, in order to break through the domination of the ruling consciousness, and in order to obtain release ever and again from the coercive mechanisms of that which is directly given and immediately reasonable, and pierce the banality of that which is.

Perhaps this will seem an unconventional or surprising interpretation of the significance of formulations of Christian belief, but I think it is cogent and compelling if we consider the peculiar situation of this present-day society in which Christian faith has to be represented. It is an increasingly a-historical society—one that is constantly losing its memory, with the result that, increasingly, traditions can be retained and brought into the present only incidentally—by means of institutions and their formulations of self-understanding, hence by means of dogmas and credal statements.

Dogmatic or confessional faith is then an affirmation of doctrines which can and must be understood as the mnemonic formulas of a repressed, unconquered, subversive and dangerous memory of humanity. A criterion of its genuine Christianity is the critical, liberating and redeeming hazardousness with which it brings the remembered Gospel into the present moment, so that men will be scandalized by it and yet be overcome by its power. Such confessional and dogmatic formulations are "dead" and "empty" when what they recall no longer displays any part of this dangerousness for society *and* for the Church! They are meaningless if this dangerousness is extinguished by the mechanisms through which they are transmitted institutionally, and if the formulas therefore serve only the self-perpetuation of the religion that has handed them on and the self-reproduction of ecclesiastical antitheses. But where the different credal expressions in Christendom persist as the remembrancers, as the orthography of a "dangerous" memory of humanity, they serve to cement and repeat not such antagonisms, but the testimony of the one Gospel of Jesus Christ. And so, perhaps, the "ecumenical" hermeneutics of the Gospel should in this present day and age be above all else a "political" hermeneutics of the Gospel: in the sense that in this hermeneutics the one Gospel in the different professions of faith will be introduced into contemporary society and its "systems" as a dangerous, liberating and redeeming *memoria Christi*.

We celebrate the Eucharist, the Lord's Supper, in our churches. We celebrate it as the *memoria Jesu Christi*, as a memorial of his death. But this means, too, that we celebrate the Lord's Supper as a memorial of his love, in which the sovereignty of God came among us in such a way that a start was made to the abolition of sovereignty among men, and that Jesus revealed himself to the dominated and enslaved, and to outcasts. Doesn't a Church of this kind, precisely for the sake of its sacramental memory, have to become the dangerously liberating sign of this love in the midst of our society? And wouldn't the Christian Churches also show a mutual increase of the unity they long for, if they saw themselves as the public representatives and bearers of this same memory?[3]

[3] More detailed observations on my *memoria* thesis in relation to Church and society are to be found in J. B. Metz, " 'Politische Theologie' in der Diskussion", in H. Peukert (ed.), *Diskussion zur "politischen Theologie"* (Mainz and Munich, 1969).

Translated by John Griffiths

Walter Kasper, Hans Küng, Johannes Remmers

5. The Extent of Convergence

I. CONVERGENCE OF ANSWERS

(*a*) The most striking characteristic of the preceding contributions on the question of a new Reformation is the departure from the straightforward abstract doctrinal point of view towards a more concrete attitude based on actual practice. Regardless of any fundamental differences which may still exist on the understanding of the ecclesiastical function of the Churches, they all apparently suffer in practice—with a remarkable degree of ecumenical unison—from clericalism and the stagnation of their institutional forms. This "negative ecumenism" not only restricts the constant reformulation and reinterpretation of the dogmas of individual Churches for the benefit and enlightenment of the others, but tends even more to have the effect of turning a particular dogma critically against the practice of its own Church. The Reformed Churches can no longer content themselves with the assurance that the Reformation is behind them; nor can the Catholic Church any longer equate the word "Reformation" with the betrayal of tradition. In the same way that the Orthodox Churches recognize that inherited orthodoxy in itself is not sufficient unless translated into reality, the Anglicans acknowledge that history does not stand still, but is making new demands of them right now. The path to Church unity can thus be found only through the renewal of the individual Churches. This insight into the historical character of truth, and the fact that it can only be brought about by means of practice, has now apparently been absorbed into the theologies of the various Churches.

(b) This unity is based on the common situation of all Churches in the universal ecumenism which is the world of today, in which the old denominational differences are of very limited interest. The questions do not relate to our increasingly subtle distinctions of doctrine, but rather to the actual nature and basis of our mutual faith—the word of God, the message of salvation through Jesus Christ. Ecumenism is concerned not so much with the actual meaning of these truths as with their relevance to the problems of peace and justice, and the freedom and happiness of humanity. The consequence of this fundamental questioning is that no Church which wishes to justify its mission can any longer afford simply to repeat the old formulas or maintain the old forms. The only way for the Churches to remain true to their mission is for them to move with the times. This mutual challenge, as well as the common experience of Christianity in an ever more unified and secularized world, produce noticeably convergent answers. Denominational differences now only play a very secondary role in the concrete questions concerning the practical realization of faith, in comparison to those differences which apply to all Churches. Hence the justification for the hope of progress through "indirect ecumenism".

(c) There is general agreement that renewal cannot be equated with innovation, and that the responsibility for the world should not be confused with any temporary adaptation to the world. Every Church admits to being bound to an obligatory tradition, and is convinced that it has something individual to contribute to the future ecumenism of both Church and humanity. Besides, the conviction is taking definite root that the Gospel can only be properly spread if preached in a truthful yet critical manner; precisely that exposure of suppressed conflicts and unsatisfied hopes can imbue the proclamation of the Gospel message with a liberating power and enable it to become of service to humanity. The memory of unresolved denominational differences—particularly if this is considered to be disturbing—could thus have the power to break the magic circle of hasty and superficial misconceptions and concentrate attention on the fundamental questions. The criterion for this would frankly be that such differences as still exist should be determined with constructive and creative intentions, rather than in any restorative or repressive way. The inflexible concept of tradition must therefore be replaced by a new understanding of tradition which recognizes that *metanoia* is demanded not only of the personal attitude of each individual Christian, but equally of the institutional attitude of the Church itself. The convergence of answers is also partly impeded by the fact that all factions are faced with equal difficulties.

II. The Convergence of Open Questions

(a) The open questions tend to stem from the essential problems themselves rather than from any diverging denominational differences, which now extend solely to the specific intensity of questioning, the level of awareness of the problems and the "local nuances" involved. Any justified emphasis of practice is by its very nature a demand for the *right* practice. Without theory "it would not be possible for practice to carry through the constant modification essential to its existence" (Th. W. Adorno). The question of truth cannot therefore be evaded. At the present moment we are faced with the even more urgent task of developing the concrete criteria for a practical historical understanding of truth; to what degree can the "world" be the criterion for Church practice, and in what way can the Gospel be the criterion for secular action? How can we hope to achieve a medium between the Scylla of the secularization of the Church and the Charybdis of the fulfilment of the world? As long as these questions go unanswered the emphasis on practice must ultimately remain in the realms of theory alone. True ecumenical theology and practice must bring us to the most fundamental of theological questions—how one can speak concretely of God and salvation in the world of today.

(b) An historical, critical and practical understanding of the truth does not touch on merely one or the other dogma or institutional form of our Church, but is essentially concerned with establishing the "scope" of the Church as a whole. The greatest differences between the so-called conservative and progressive groups to be found in all Churches today lie not so much in divergent views on any specific questions (viz., liturgical reform, historical criticism in biblical research, social involvement, and so on), but rather in their totally different basic attitudes. It can therefore be said to be a question of overall mentality. Only by recognizing this universal character of the problems of ecclesiastical reform can we really appreciate the extent of the revolutionary changes now taking effect. In such a situation there is no point whatever in minor alterations or "patching up": for only that faith has comprehended the sign of the times which dares not merely to look over the denominational barriers and perhaps exchange a few neighbourly words, but which dares to jump right over them. In this sort of situation, integral and clerical rigidity could almost amount to a kind of constitutional unbelief.

The extensive character of the reforms vital to all Churches shows that none of the above-mentioned opinions succeeds in suggesting an even moderately concrete concept of a renewed open Church. In addition to the freedom necessary for responsible experimentation, what we stand in most need of in this period of transition is a faith which can right now trust blindly in the power of the Spirit. Claudel once said that the word of God was not like a restricted searchlight illuminating a certain point ahead of us, but like an undying torch which throws light everywhere around us only as we move forward.

Translated by Sarah O'Brien-Twohig

Gotthold Hasenhüttl

Confessional Aspects in Contemporary Theology
1. The Question about God

I. THE QUESTION ABOUT GOD—ROOT CAUSE OF DENOMINATIONAL DIFFERENCES?

WE are all familiar with the line of argument which runs: denominational differences must be grasped by their roots; granted that we differ in the way we look at the sacraments, this is, however, basically a question of our understanding of the Church. And this can only be cleared up if light is shed on the deepseated christological differences which must be settled. These in turn reveal an essentially different doctrine of the Trinity which, in the final analysis, is rooted in a false or one-sided notion of God—and here the rift between the two sides allows no passage from one to the other. In sacramental theology it may still be possible to bridge the gulf of controversy, but no way across can be found where the dispute is about God himself.

These profound thoughts are, however, for the most part too profound: concentrating on the deepest roots of doctrinal difference, they pass entirely over what lies nearer the surface. Ecumenists who think in this way are like a chemist who knows all about the chemical changes that occur when he cooks a pot of pea soup, but then forgets to turn the gas down at the right time, with the result that the soup gets burnt, and he is left with an empty stomach. In my opinion, many disputes can be effectively dealt with without touching the question about God. That is not, of course, to say that these questions do not hang together, but only that we are faced here with a reciprocal process, not with a sort of one-way street argument that makes it imperative to start with the God-question. For example, the matter of justification can be settled before our question is finally mastered, though naturally the light shed on justification will clarify the problem about God, and vice versa.

A phenomenology of the God-question soon brings denominational factors to light. Since 1960, when the problem about God was again taken up intensively, it has been mainly Protestant theologians who have concerned themselves with it. And they have shown a marked tendency towards anthropology in theology: one could cite, for instance, the American "God-is-dead" theology, or J. A. T. Robinson in England, or, in Germany, H. Braun and D. Sölle with their circle. In the Catholic world there has been no outstanding attempt to open up new paths into the question, in a way that would do justice to the concerns of those Protestant theologians.

This new wave of Protestant thought on the subject was set in motion by the dialectical thought of the 1930s, where, in conversations with Catholic theologians such as E. Przywara and others, and in discussions between Protestants themselves (e.g., Karl Barth and Emil Brunner: the controversy about *"theologia naturalis"*!) unique emphasis was laid on the absolute sovereignty of God. As "totally other" he was almost pushed away into the realm of pure transcendence. Protestant God-talk seems to be particularly strongly exposed to this dichotomy between pure this-worldliness and pure other-worldliness with regard to God. It threatens to fall from one extreme into the other, while its Catholic counterpart follows its course at a peaceful, measured pace. What lies behind this?

We must first of all make it quite clear that at the time of the Reformation nobody on either side expressed or even entertained doubts about the existence of God. As in biblical times, God's existence was self-evident and not open to discussion. Everybody understood the word "God". The Trinity, too, and the Incarnation of God's Son were, in the sixteenth century, acknowledged as facts almost without dispute. And every present-day theologian too will, in so far as he is still "one who talks about God" (theo-logian), still speaks of the existence of God. But in doing so he will be well aware that naïvety is no longer tolerable, and the time has passed when the idea of God could be taken as self-evident. So it is that today even the death of God can marginally be thought possible, though none of the theologians we have mentioned would take this to mean a simple atheistic denial of God.

The problem has shifted. It is no longer a question of accepting God's existence as known, and commenting on *how* he exists, but of standing, so to speak, at the horizon of godlessness and searching through space and time for that place *where* the reality might come to light which men will dare to call by the name of "God". This new question about God has not dropped out of the blue on to our generation: it showed at least a partial presence at the outbreak of the Reformation and of the modern era.

How, then, does God stand towards men?

II. KNOWLEDGE OF GOD IN BEING OR IN FAITH?

God is not far distant from the man who knows him—that is the Thomist tradition up till the First Vatican Council. This nearness is grounded in the sharing of being (*S. Th.*, I, 3, 4; I, 7, 1; I, 75, 5, *ad* 4). Transcendence is proclaimed in the ontological difference between man's nature and his being (cf. *Quodl.*, III, q. 8, a. 20). Being, in the existent, that is, in man, proclaims God and is therefore a way to him. We know the famous five ways of reaching knowledge of God, at the end of which Thomas concludes: and that *all men* call God (*S. Th.*, I, 2, 3). All that is has been founded by God, has him as its creator. Man has an analogical knowledge of this God who is the root of all that is—not a knowledge that reduces the question about him to silence, but one that does bring a certain nearness to him. It is not as though man could talk *about* God, for the simple reason that he has no horizon which could include God in its sweep; but what *is* possible is a speaking *out to* God. Already before St Thomas's time the Church was aware of an analogous knowledge of God: a knowledge which, far from blotting out the distinction between God and creatures, serves rather to emphasize his enormous difference from them. So it is that the Fourth Lateran Council pointed out that the similarity between God and man is far smaller than their difference (DB 432). This certain "similarity" is still maintained in principle despite the fact that the Council was speaking here of the Trinity; "natural knowledge of God" was not directly under dispute. Not until the First Vatican Council do we hear expressly that the one true God, our Creator and Lord, can be known with certainty through what exists, by the natural light of human reason (DB 1806).

It must be observed that only the basic possibility of knowing God is spoken of here. Whether the possibility is ever realized remains an open question. All that is asserted is man's fundamental ability, not extinguished even in the realm of sin, to have this knowledge. And the Council Fathers were not talking either about a purely theoretical knowledge of God which would prescind from the operation of man's will.

To Protestants, this preoccupation is incomprehensible, if not suspect, for it seems to play down the distance between sinful man and God. For all that, however, it is not certain that Luther himself denied that men could get to know God by their natural powers or by force of Tradition,[1] as has been maintained by some theologians.[2] He seems to have considered knowledge of God's being to be possible, but not knowledge of his will. Calvin too, with his basic training in Thomistic scholasticism, speaks of a *"duplex cognitio Domini"*.[3] By his very nature, man can have an effective knowledge of God. Certainly this is, for Calvin, only possible in principle: it cannot be realized in practice. But it is objectively possible in principle. It is, I think, questionable whether Calvin really differs from Vatican I on this point, for there too the bishops spoke only of the objective possibility. So, according to Calvin, knowledge of God in Christ includes an effective knowledge of God through creation. It is certainly hard to tell to what extent knowledge of God through created being is for Calvin more than an abstract possibility, whereas for Vatican I it was also a concrete one. For he goes on to say *"si integer stetisset Adam"* (Institut., I, 2. 1). Real knowledge of God is, for him, always born of obedience (*Institut.*, I, 6, 2). It is, then, as

[1] Thus G. Ebeling, "Luthers Reden von Gott", in *Der Gottesgedanke im Abendland* (Stuttgart, 1964), p. 36.
[2] W. Pannenberg, "Gott", in *RGG*, p. 1726.
[3] *Institut.*, I, 2, 1; *Conf. Gall.*, 1559, art. 2.

true for him as for Luther, that God's will can only be known in the acceptance of revelation.

In the light of this analysis, hard as it is to clarify, it is no wonder that Brunner appeals to Calvin for a *"theologia naturalis"*,[4] and Karl Barth, referring to the same Calvin, answers him with a trenchant "No".[5] In Barth's opinion it is precisely this opposition of Protestant theology to the Catholic sort of knowledge of God that must not be done away with, even if it is not expressed very clearly in the Reformers themselves (cf., *ibid.*, p. 38). Against Brunner he writes: "Really to reject natural theology is not like gazing at the serpent only to be hypnotized by a return stare and then bitten—rather, in the very moment you first catch sight of it you have already beaten it with your stick, and beaten it to death! . . . Real rejection of natural theology can only be brought about in fear of God, and so in *not* being interested in this matter at all" (*ibid.*, p. 13).

Brunner, on the other hand, basing himself on Romans 1. 19 f., tries to show that even outside the historical revelation man forms an idea of God, and "sinful man . . . [is] responsible for his sin because in creation there is a revelation which enables him to get to know God".[6]

Without going into all the details now, we can see that denominational factors do indeed come into the question of knowledge of God, but that they do not necessarily find their origin in different communities. F. Buri sums the matter up very well: "The realization that the world is God's creation and the object of his providence is in principle ascribed to reason as well as to revelation. *How* this is so is, on the other hand, reserved to supernatural revelation. The Catholic Church, referring to the Bible, acknowledges this rational knowledge, but the Reformers, notably Luther, had reservations about it. Both points of view are represented in more recent Protestant theology: that God can only be known from his revelation in Christ, and that in the

---

[4] E. Brunner, *Natur und Gnade, Zum Gespräch mit K. Barth* (Zürich, 1934).—Translated along with Barth's reply *Nein!* as E. Brunner, *Natural Theology* (London, 1956).

[5] *Nein! Antwort an E. Brunner* (Zürich, 1934). Cf. footnote 4 above for English translation.

[6] E. Brunner, *The Christian Doctrine of God, Dogmatics*, vol. I (London, 1949), p. 66.

matter of knowledge of God nothing is valid if it cannot prove itself before the bar of reason."[7]

Protestant theology, however, does seem to be agreed on one point: if he does not accept God's Word in faith, man, for all his knowledge of God, lives at an absolute distance from him. The greater weight put by Catholics on knowledge of God, even for faith, is unmistakable, in spite of their conviction that real knowledge of God is attained only by those who live in his love.

One must then say that a valid proof of God's existence cannot save man from himself, or be of any benefit to him.[8] And nowadays this particular question about knowledge of God has been almost entirely forgotten, although the after-effects of the various views still make themselves clearly felt.

III. GOD OF ORDER OR GOD OF HISTORY?

Realizing that the only true approach to God is through Christ, Catholic thought on the subject has always tried to penetrate the reality of God from the standpoint of God-as-revealed. As we have seen, the official magisterium has never concerned itself with a closer intellectual penetration of the reality of God (the concern of Vatican I in this respect is no more than general, cf. DB 1782, 1805); all its statements have been of a brief, unsystematic and occasional nature. Starting from man's analogical knowledge of God, theologians have tried to show how God, in his freedom, has committed himself to the world in the act of creation. In this way, creatures too are given greater value, for the God of the cosmos shows himself in them: God is a God of order and not of chaos. The whole order of the world and of salvation has its origins in him, and that precisely as one total *ordo*. An appeal to the fundamental quality of this concept of order certainly reaches the heart of the medieval idea of God, and to some extent the heart of the modern Catholic idea too. Everything begins from God and has its rightful place from him—a place which man, in his turn, must not leave; and all returns to find in him its home and its fulfilment. Only in God can the

---

[7] *Unterricht im christlichen Glauben* (Berne, 1957), pp. 58-9.
[8] Cf. J.-P. Sartre, *Existentialism and Humanism* (London, 1948).

Whole be understood, and its sense be grasped. Even salvation history is, in fact, less a narrative existing at the level of ordinary history than a salvific ordering of history which shares in the existence of God. God's activity in his creation is all-powerful, direct and free; but it is not arbitrary. Nor is he, *pace* Aristotle, merely the final cause who, like a magnet, draws all creation to himself, yet in himself remains unmoved; he is not like a woman who holds coldly aloof from the lover whose passion she has roused. On the contrary, he has turned in love to his creation, and imprinted on it his eternal order, so that it may find salvation.

For St Thomas, the whole world-order is in this way the created fulfilment of God's will: of his will to grant a sharing in his being and order his creatures to himself (1 *Sent.*, d. 39, q. 2, a, 1; *S. Th.*, I, 19, 5). In this *ordinatio Dei*, the question of deviant action by God is a pure abstraction: even his will can be known through creation. For God is truth and faithfulness; the pledge of his steadfastness lies in his very being: a being which is, however, not dead but alive and imprinted with the vital stamp of knowledge and will. The one being which exists of and in itself (*ipsum esse subsistens*) is full of life and vitality: God's stillness is not the stillness of the grave. So it is that man can worship and believe in him, the eternal one, who does not pass away.

Augustine, too, thinks of God along these lines: everything is changeable, so man reaches out beyond himself in search of the unchangeable, and in this way attains to knowledge of God (cf. *Hom.*, 241, 2–3). "How then 'is' it—that which does not stand fast? Yet it 'is', for it comes and it goes. I seek what simply and plainly 'is'; I seek what truly 'is'; I seek what really 'is'" (*In Ps.*, 38. 8). Or, as St Thomas says: "Now since it is God's nature to exist, he it must be who properly causes existence in creatures ... not just when they begin to exist, but all the time they are maintained in existence, just as the sun is lighting up the atmosphere all the time the atmosphere remains lit.... Now existence is more intimately and profoundly interior to things than anything else, for everything is potential when compared to existence. So God must exist and exist intimately in every-thing.... The perfection of his nature places God above everything, and yet as causing their existence he also exists

in everything. . . . God contains things by existing in them"
(*S. Th.*, I, 8, 1—Translation by T. McDermott, o.p.; *Blackfriars*,
1964).

Something of this train of thought seems to be present in the
question about God even today. It is not entirely for nothing that
Catholics are said to have a far more firmly orientated sense of
direction in this matter, though that can indeed easily lead to
complacency and false feelings of security.

Luther experienced the downfall of the concept of order about
which we have been speaking. For him, only personal faith be-
stows certainty that God's voice is speaking; and to talk about
God is to assume a personal responsibility. Faced with faith, all
ideas of a world-order crumble away. God and faith go together,
and do so exclusively. Thus Luther can begin his exposition of
the First Commandment in the *Grosser Katechismus* ("Great
Catechism"): "It says one God so that men shall look confidently
to him for all good things and turn to him in every need. So to
have one God is nothing other than to have heartfelt trust and
faith in him. I have often said in this way that the heart's trust
and faith alone makes both God and idol. Your God is true if
your faith and trust are true, and conversely, if trust is false and
unjustified the real God is not there. For the two belong together,
faith and God. He then in reality is your God . . . on whom you
fix your heart, in whom you trust" (*W.A.*, 30, 1; 132, 32–133, 8
[1529]). This immediate proximity of the believer to God can
easily lead to a false shifting of God's reality on to the believing
subject, so that God becomes the self-projection of man, and theology dissolves into anthropology (Feuerbach). It is, of course,
equally wrong to turn these ideas into so theocentric a system
that man, as it were, fades away into nothingness in relation to
God. Both these tendencies find a foothold in Luther's highly
wrought thinking, whereas in the Catholic world they do not,
on the whole, so easily come by their nourishment.

On the other hand an essential step is taken here to eradicate all
frivolity from talk about God; he is understood and spoken of as
simply and solely the one who has concern for and approaches
man. God is here the reality to which man is attracted, with an
attraction that bids fair to change his situation (one of need), in

so far as it puts him in a new relationship with it. Further, talking about God is seen as talking about an *event*: that of God establishing a rapport with the believer. So God's being is, for men, always a "possessing of God": God is always God-for-me. And knowledge of God is brought into the context of human self-knowledge: the two form, broadly speaking, one event. The attempt is made to consider God and World together, and as it were to draw them closer to each other. God is himself bound in with history, and he enters into a vital exchange with the man who believes. He is not merely there as the root of being and its end (egress-regress), but is there for me in the unfolding of history. According to G. Ebeling, God comes as fellow man into the world in the very fact of man's "being-in-the-world"—a state that is signalled out by its unfulfilled need for fellowship; for man is the "image and likeness of God who is his fellow" (*ibid.*, p. 52).

From these indications we can see that present-day currents of thought about God are concerned especially with the attempt to bring God into the process of history and yet to let him still be God. E. Przywara, in his writings on the philosophy of religion (Einsiedeln, 1962), tried around the 1930s to put the question in the following way, without being able to solve it: God is all *in* all, and all *beyond* all, "his immanence (*Inne-Sein*) in every creature is the revelation of his infinite transcendence (*Über-Sein*). *Deus exterior et interior*. God in us and beyond us" (p. 280). We know the various Catholic and Protestant formulations on this point: God *becomes* in relationship with what is other (*Gott wird am anderen*) (K. Rahner); God's being is in becoming (E. Jungel). These expressions affirm God's existence, as was done by medieval man, but they want at the same time to bring God conceptually into history, into space and time.

We can see how denominational factors in the question about God reflect the various currents of our Western thought. A simple either-or would foreshorten the whole idea of God.

God in himself—God for me; God as eternal—God as entering time; we men are continually faced with these apparent contradictions. But we shall only fall prey to one-sidedness and over-simplification if we make an absolute of one pole of the discussion and exclude the other. Catholics and Protestants all face the same reality; they approach it by paths that are equally difficult; and they give it the same name—God, the Father of our Lord Jesus Christ.

Translated by J. T. Swann

Hans Grass

Confessional Aspects in Contemporary Theology
2. The Question about Christ

I. The Christology of the Reformers in Relation to the Traditional Teaching

LUTHER's Schmalkalden Articles of 1537 are a constituent element of the Lutheran *corpus* of writings. He explains there at the end of Section I, which deals very concisely with the Trinity and the Son of God: "These Articles are subject to no quarrel nor dispute, because on either side we [believe and] confess the same." He in fact struck out the words "believe and" from his original draft, because he did not consider Catholics capable of true faith. And he marked down as the main point of controversy the first article of the next section. It deals with the ministry and work of Christ and with our salvation, culminating in the doctrine of justification by faith alone without the works of the Law.[1] In the Augsburg Confession of 1530, the basic confession of the Reform, Melanchthon could compose the article about the Son of God (art. III) in a way that harmonized with the teaching of the Catholic Church: the Son of God took to himself the nature of man in the Virgin Mary, so that two natures are inseparably joined together in one person. To this statement he attached a paraphrase of the christological part of the Apostles' Creed. And even those who would have the Augsburg Confession proven false, made clear that they found nothing offensive in its third article.[2] Of course they prescinded here from the question about Christ's

[1] *Bekenntnisschriften* of the Lutheran Church (1930), p. 415.
[2] *Corpus Reformatorum*, XXVII, col. 90 f.

work, and confined their judgment to the teaching about his person. To Luther, heresy about the person of Christ was the lesser of two evils, compared with heresy about his work. And in the same way, Melanchthon, in the fourth article, "On Justification", of the Apology for the Augsburg Confession, repeatedly reproached its adversaries with being ignorant of Christ and with doing him an outrage by their false understanding of his saving work.[3] If we were to deal with our question on the basis of the Reformation controversies, we should have to discuss this agreement in christology in the narrow sense, along with the disagreement in soteriology, or christology in the broader sense. And as these two areas of doctrine are correlative, many interesting points would arise. The fact remains that even today Protestant christology is still characterized by its soteriological tendency.

II. Differing Present-day Attitudes to the Dogma of Christ

Since the sixteenth century, however, there has been a development in the field of christology which we cannot pass over in silence; and in respect of this development, Protestant theology has undergone a far greater change than has taken place in Catholic theology. Briefly, christology in the narrower sense, the teaching about the person of Christ, has become a matter for controversy within the Protestant communion. The doctrine of the two natures in Christ, the dogma of Chalcedon, has found more critics than supporters; nor is the *"homoousios"* of Nicaea beyond dispute. The line of critics extends from Schleiermacher to Ritschl and Harnack, and then on to Bultmann and Gogarten. The line of those who defend the ancient dogmas, held in the nineteenth century first and foremost by the conservative "confessing" tradition in theology, has in our own time found powerful and effective representation above all in Karl Barth. But the Lutheran Werner Elert and the earlier Emil Brunner must also be counted as defenders, as well as the Barthian Heinrich Vogel. Barth derived his teaching on the Trinity, and with it some of the essential statements of his christology, from an unfolding of the idea of revelation. But it is none the less characteristic that most Protestant

[3] *Bekenntnisschriften*, p. 170, line 1 f., 30 f.; p. 176, line 29 f.; p. 181, line 13 f.; p. 189, line 36 f.; p. 190, line 17 f.

defenders of the ancient christological dogmas take Jesus as their starting-point, or the New Testament witness to Christ, and from this starting-point they attempt to derive the dogma's assertions as necessary theological consequences. This method accords with the Protestant view of the relationship between Scripture and Tradition, a view which plays a considerable part in the denominational aspect of our theme.

The Second Vatican Council's Decree on Ecumenism was clearly referring to the basic formula drawn up by the World Council of Churches when it gave the name "brother Christians" to those from the separated Churches and ecclesial communities of the West "who openly confess Jesus Christ as God and Lord and as the sole mediator between God and man". But the same passage goes on to say "that among them views are held considerably different from the doctrine of the Catholic Church even concerning Christ, God's Word made flesh, and the work of redemption, and thus concerning the mystery and ministry of the Church and the role of Mary in the work of salvation". And then, at least in the final redaction of the Council text, all these separated brethren are granted is that they are " 'looking to' Christ (*in Christum intendere*—Trans.) as the source and centre of ecclesiastical communion". The text does not allow of any more precise definition of where the christological differences lie. One cannot tell whether the Council Fathers have in mind rather the old soteriological dispute of Reformation times, or differences that have arisen from modern Protestant dogma-criticism. But the discussion of this paragraph of the Decree does stress the point that those who deny the divinity of Christ can only be called Christians in a very analogical sense.[4] The Council did have a plan to refute doctrinal errors in the field of christology as well, but the project was dropped after the first session, and whether it would have dealt with Protestant views or confined itself to deciding controversies within the Catholic fold, is something that lies beyond my knowledge. But the christological passage in Section 20 of the Decree on Ecumenism is in any case characteristic in the way it speaks in one breath of Christ, his work, the

[4] Cf. Lorenz Cardinal Jaeger, *Das Konzilsdekret "Über den Ökumenismus* (Paderborn, 1965), p. 136.—Translated as *A Stand on Ecumenism: the Council's Decree* (London, 1965).

Church, and Mary. A. Grillmeier makes clear right at the beginning of his essay "Zum Christusbild der heutigen katholischen Theologie"[5] ("Christ in Modern Catholic Theology") that in Catholic theology Christ, Mary and the Church form an "inseparable unity . . . like concentric circles belonging in the one order of the incarnation". Later on[6] he describes Christ, the Church and the sacraments as an inseparable whole—Christ's becoming man was not just a phase in history, its significance is eternal. The idea of the primal sacrament (*Ursakrament*) has also been used to link up these three doctrinal peaks; but that idea is foreign to Protestant theology. If Christ is associated there with any one means of grace, it is with the Word. The sacraments are understood from the point of view of the Word; the Church is understood as Christ's servant and servant of the Word. The tendency to look on the Church as *Christus prolongatus* is almost entirely rejected by Protestant theology.

III. Attempts to go beyond Early-Church Dogma

This is, of course, not to say that Catholic christology has been stationary: the publications on the occasion of the jubilee of Chalcedon have shown that.[7] While some theologians, either from the point of view of the history of dogma or from that of dogmatic theology itself, expounded the Chalcedonian definition as the fundamental christological dogma of the Church, others wanted to go beyond Chalcedon. Karl Rahner's essay *Chalkedon —Ende oder Anfang?*[8] ("Chalcedon—End or Beginning?") best represents these. Rahner points out with some clarity that the dogma is very scanty in comparison with the christology of the Bible: a more biblical approach, he thinks, is called for.[9] And

[5] In *Fragen der Theologie heute*, ed. Feiner, Trütsch, Böckle (1957), pp. 265 f.—Translated as *Theology Today* (Milwaukee, 1965).

[6] *Ibid.*, p. 271.

[7] Cf. the three-volume collection: *Das Konzil von Chalkedon*, ed. A. Grillmeier and H. Bacht (1951–54).

[8] *Ibid.*, III, pp. 3–49.

[9] Cf. A. Grillmeier, *Zum Christusbild der heutigen katholischen Theologie*, p. 266: "Teaching about Christ has been committed in too one-sided a fashion to the well-known formulas of the ancient Councils, and theologians have consequently been prevented from exploiting to the full the rich biblical image of Christ, or even from taking note of the basic features of this image."

indeed Catholic theologians have taken important steps in this direction in dogmatic theology as well as in exegesis. This is above all evident in the way ideas have been taken up from salvation hisory,[10] and greater stress laid on the manhood of Christ, and on the life of Jesus as one lived in free obedience in the sight of God.

In this context the demand has also been made that more attention be given to the doctrine about Christ's condition, that is, the way of self-emptying (*kenosis*—Trans.) and exaltation, as opposed to the teaching about his two natures.[11]

These salvation history ideas have left their mark on some of the central statements in the Second Vatican Council's Constitution on the Church. And the christology of the Dutch Catechism (*A New Catechism*), leaning heavily on the Gospel reports, simply portrays the Son of Man's passage from his origins through to his exaltation.

It is, however, interesting for the Protestant observer to see that the most important problems in Catholic christology are still conditioned by the teaching about the two natures in Christ. This is most of all true in the much-discussed question about the psychology of Christ.[12] Déodat de Basly and Galtier first broached the question about the autonomy of Jesus in the life of his human soul—an issue which has even given rise to an official attitude being taken up by the Church's magisterium.

This question does not coincide with the one put in Protestant research circles about Jesus' self-consciousness and his consciousness as Messiah. Discussion of this latter point is dying out nowadays, because theologians have learnt to distinguish between an implicit or explicit claim to be Messiah, and consciousness as Messiah. It was conditioned by the critico-historical question about the actual claims of the historical Jesus himself; for it is clear that the christological nature of the Gospel tradition about

---

[10] Cf., for example, Y. Congar, "Christ in the Economy of Salvation and in our Dogmatic Tracts", in *Concilium*, Jan. 1966 (American edn., vol. 11).

[11] Cf. P. Schoonenberg, "The Kenosis or Self-Emptying of Christ", in *Concilium*, Jan. 1966 (American edn., vol. 11).

[12] Cf. Grillmeier, *op. cit.*, pp. 277 f., where the question about Christ's consciousness is described as the most recent and most important question in modern christology, pp. 296 f. Joseph Ternus, "Das Seelen- und Bewusstsein Jesu", in *Das Konzil von Chalkedon*, vol. III, pp. 81–237. K. Rahner, *Theological Investigations*, V, pp. 193–215.

Jesus is largely the work of the post-Resurrection community. Catholic treatment of Christ's psychology, on the other hand, is dominated by the question as to how his full, omniscient, divine nature is related to his limited human nature. Theologians try, so far as they can, to do justice to the self-sufficiency of the man Jesus, in the light of the predominance given officially to the *Logos*. Rahner posits an absolute basic state in Jesus of being directly present to God, a consciousness of being God's Son that is compatible with a truly human spiritual history and development of the beatific vision of God.[13] But this idea, too, is rather a speculative construction than a development taken from the Gospel tradition about Jesus, or from the New Testament proclamation of Christ.

And this is even more the case with the evolutionary, cosmic christology initiated by Teilhard de Chardin and developed by various Catholic theologians, among them Karl Rahner[14] and H. Riedlinger.[15] Rahner wants to grasp not only the whole movement of history, but also the evolution of the cosmos, as a process centred on the incarnation of God, an entelechy striving towards Christ. He sees the history of the world and of the spirit as the history of a self-transcendence into the life of God—a self-transcendence which, in its final and highest phase, is identical with an absolute self-communication of God.[16]

The idea of the Saviour contains implicitly that of the hypostatic unity of God and man, a unity for which the relation of God to man as creator to creature forms the *analogia entis* (analogy of being). Rahner constructs this idea in a speculative fashion, and sees it finally as realized concretely in Christ. He does indeed stress that the notion of a possible incarnation could be drawn so clearly from a formal scheme of world-evolution if we did not already know of the actual incarnation.[17] He sees, too, that within the framework of evolutionary, cosmic theology

[13] *Ibid*., pp. 211 f.
[14] K. Rahner, "Christology within an Evolutionary View of the World", in *Theological Investigations*, V, pp. 157–92.
[15] H. Riedlinger, "How Universal is Christ's Kingship?", in *Concilium*, Jan. 1966 (American edn., vol. 11).
[16] *Op. cit*., pp. 178–9.
[17] *Ibid*., p. 187.

serious problems arise about sin, guilt and salvation,[18] and about eschatology.[19] But all the same, this christological theory can, he believes, be worked out in a meaningful way. It is reminiscent of nineteenth-century speculative christology, which had come under the influence of Hegel and Schelling, been sharply criticized by Kierkegaard, and been turned against its authors by the left-wing Hegelians Strauss and Feuerbach. Modern Protestant theology views such attempts as this with great reserve.

Riedlinger indeed does see recent Protestant theology as using the cosmic christology of the letters to the Ephesians and Colossians in an effort to relax the centuries-old anthropocentric fixation of Protestant christology. He points out that it was not for nothing that the representatives of the young African and Asian Churches at New Delhi protested against the neglect of the cosmic dimension of Jesus Christ.[20] But then he is himself forced to state that an exegete like Conzelmann interprets these cosmic ideas, influenced by gnosticism, in an anthropological way. Such interpretations are not rooted merely in the realization that modern man does not take kindly to the cosmic mythology of gnosticism, nor do they merely result from the concentration on sin and grace in the Western Reformation; they belong rather in the context of that understanding of the world which modern Protestantism sees as having been determined by scientific research.

A theology at grips with the problem of forming a unified vision of God and this "godless" world is not inclined to start speculating about a cosmic Christ, the embodiment of an incarnational principle gratuitously predicated of the evolution of the world. Paul Tillich's christology too, although embedded in a comprehensive ontology, does remain closer to the historical Christ of the Bible; and moreover it makes use of a notion of symbol that cripples the binding force of its speculative assertions. Nor does the greater attention paid by modern Protestant theology to the Kingdom of God and the Kingdom of Christ do anything to alter Protestant aversion to evolutionary cosmic christology although it does open up the narrow individualism of their

---

[18] *Ibid.*, pp. 184 f.
[19] *Ibid.*, pp. 188 f.
[20] *Op. cit.*, p. 57.

outlook on salvation. The great ecumenical conferences[21] were concerned to relate the reign of Christ to our historical and social world; they were not concerned with cosmological speculations. Their tendency, too, was man-centred; not indeed centred on the salvation of the individual, but on the well-being and future of human society.

There is no lack in Catholic theology, either, of voices calling for a change of emphasis in christology: for a change from cosmic questions about the totality of being (*all-kosmische Seinsfrage*) to human questions about the totality of us men (*all-menschliche Wirfrage*). They start from the idea of sharing human fellowship as a basic experience and as a general limit to experience. From this idea they want to achieve an understanding of Jesus first and foremost as fellow man and as man-for-others. They feel an urgent need for a theology of the cross, a need which has not till now been adequately met in Catholic circles.[22] But in fact here, too, despite all their criticism of classical theology for being impregnated with the Greek notion of being, they are only demanding in the final analysis that the traditional christology, with its concentration on questions about being, should be completed in a christology centred on us men.[23]

Even this attempt, then, ends in the "both . . . and" so characteristic of all Catholic efforts at renewal. This "both . . . and" is rooted in the way one looks at the relationship between Scripture and Tradition—rooted, in other words, in the definitive binding power of the Church's christological dogma. It is perhaps true that Catholic christology tends to stress the incarnation rather than the cross, but some Protestant schemes have a similar stress, although they do avoid extending the idea of incarnation to the Church and her sacramental means of grace. One can say that so far as the relationship between actualism/functionalism and ontology is concerned, the relationship between existential and

[21] O. Rousseau refers to them in his essay, "The Idea of the Kingship of Christ", in *Concilium*, Jan. 1966 (American edn., vol. 11).

[22] H. Mühlen, "Christologie im Horizont der Traditionellen Seinsfrage?", in *Catholica*, 23 (1969), pp. 205–39, polemically sub-titled "Towards a Theology of the Cross—a Dispute with the Traditional Christology."

[23] *Ibid.*, p. 238.

essential statements, Catholic theology has always stood for the necessity of ontological, essential statements. Bultmann's question: "Does Christ help me because he is the Son of God, or is he the Son of God because he helps me?" always receives an affirmative answer from Catholics to its first part.[24]

But Protestant christology too has many voices which reject an exclusive actualism or functionalism. One need only point to the christocentric nature of Protestant theology, which in Karl Barth mounts to the point of monism.[25] On the other hand one can find a strong christocentric stress in Catholic theology too; and Barth's christomonism, which is unacceptable to Catholics, is also rejected on good grounds by many Protestant theologians.

In my opinion, the various emphases in this matter are less important than the attitude taken to the dogma about Christ. The questions put in Protestant theology go back from the dogma to the Scriptures. And then, faced with the diverse nature of the New Testament witness to Christ, this theology does not look to dogma for a unifying centre, but continues searching back to what lies behind the New Testament evidence. So christology is taken back to its beginnings, either in Jesus, or in the Christ-event, or in the primitive *kerygma*; and then from there the attempt is made to see how present-day man can aptly express his witness to Christ. That gives christology, at least to a degree, a radically critical character, which sometimes threatens to dissolve it altogether, as is perhaps the case with Herbert Braun. At all events it leads to very different christological schemes.

Catholic theology also appeals to Scripture, but in view of the diversity of the biblical evidence—and no contradictions are admitted in this evidence—it finds its centre of unity in the dogma established by the Church; and this, in the last analysis, is seen to be in agreement with the Scriptures. This being the case, limits

[24] Cf. R. Schnackenburg, "Der Abstand der christologischen Aussagen des neuen Testaments vom chalkedonischen Bekenntnis nach der Deutung Rudolf Bultmanns" (The distance between the christological statements of the New Testament and the Chalcedonian Confession of Faith, according to the interpretation of R. Bultmann), in *Das Konzil von Chalkedon*, III, p. 684; cf., too, Y. Congar: *Christ in the Economy of Salvation*, pp. 8 f.

[25] Dorothee Sölle also in a certain way stands for an extreme christocentrism, with her christology of the representative after the death of God, though this christocentrism does then shift from concentration on Jesus our fellow man to fellowship itself.

are set in the field of criticism too, be this historical, exegetical or dogmatic. So it is that Protestant christology, with all its diversity and inner conflict, is faced with an equally differentiated Catholic theology, but one which is fundamentally united, and which does indeed owe to Protestant theology a good deal of the stimulation which has recently aroused it.

IV. Differences in Devotion to Christ

Unfortunately the restricted space allotted to this essay does not allow of more detailed treatment of the differences in devotion to Christ. Friedrich Heiler once remarked that the Christ of Catholic apologetics and doctrine is different from the Christ of actual piety.[26] Protestant devotion to Christ is basically a piety of the Word. Luther's saying: "Christ comes to us in the Gospel" still holds good today.[27] But for him the Gospel is in dialectical tension with the Law, a fact that is not always noticed in modern Protestant theology of the Word. The second major influence in Protestant piety is the Gospel picture of Jesus: a picture of the earthly Lord which corresponds and unites with the message from the cross. The centre-point of Catholic piety is Christ's presence in the Church's liturgy: the eucharistic Christ, offering himself in the Mass, worshipped in the reservation and exposition of the Blessed Sacrament.

Devotion to Jesus is largely expressed by way of imitating Christ; devotion to the Passion is cultivated by the Stations of the Cross and other ceremonies, and not least by means of the crucifix. The cult of the Sacred Heart gives rise to devotional practices very varied in their quality. Nor can Protestants overlook the Marian element in Catholic piety, in its relationship to the christological and eucharistic elements which it accompanies. This devotion to Mary has found expression in all sorts of different forms, and it is today harder than ever to say where exactly its heart is to be found.

[26] F. Heiler, *Der Katholizismus. Seine Idee und seine Erscheinung* (1923), p. 354.
[27] For example, Weimarer Ausgabe, 10, III, p. 349, line 17; p. 210, line 11; p. 92, line 11.

Translated by J. T. Swann

Albert van den Heuvel

Confessional Aspects in Contemporary Theology
3. Church and the World

I. The Churches meet the World

BASIC to all theological debates of our time is the search for the right relation of the Church to the rest of the world. *Gaudium et Spes* was a symbol for much joy and even more hope. As Cardinal Centro stated when introducing *Lumen Gentium* to the third session of the Second Vatican Council: "No other document aroused so much interest and raised so many hopes."[1] In the history of the renewal of the Roman Catholic Church it meant a turning-point: from then on the road the Church chooses through history looks quite different.

At the Fourth Assembly of the World Council of Churches the same subject was central[2] but it did not represent such a turning-point: in the ecumenical movement the question of the Church in the world has been the main concern of the member Churches of the WCC ever since 1948. In that year the "Life and Work" and "Faith and Order" movements were amalgamated: concerns for social action and political witness were married to the search for the restoration of the unity of the Church.

The amalgamation was not unpremeditated, and neither did it occur without criticism![3] Already in the nineteenth century, and even more so in the first five decades of the twentieth, the question of world and Church was raised. The lay movements,

---

[1] Xavier Rynne, *The Third Session* (London, 1964), p. 117.
[2] See Norman Goodall, *The Uppsala Report* (Geneva, 1968), p. xvii.
[3] Neill and Rouse, *The History of the Ecumenical Movement* (London, 1954), chap. 16.

grandparents of the WCC, were based on a combination of pene-
trating social engagement and an element of deep personal faith.[4]
The modern missionary movement was possible because a few
pioneers discovered that a divided Church contradicts its own
mission. "Life and Work" may have started from rather naïve
presuppositions ("The world is too strong for a divided Church"
and "Service unites; doctrine divides"). We should not forget that
the same people who led "Life and Work" were also active in
"Faith and Order" and vice versa. The reason is simple: the search
for organic unity in the Church is doomed to fail if it is not a
search for pro-existential unity. And also: common witness and
service run the danger of shallowness and syncretism if they do
not provide the context and the reason for theological activity.
The modern ecumenical movement was made possible by the
acceptance of the interpenetration of these three important elements: unity, witness and service.

With the establishment of the World Council of Churches, the
double emphasis on "Life and Work" and "Faith and Order"
has instigated the beginnings of a new way of Christian life and
a new way of Christian thinking. This process was enhanced and
deepened considerably when the Roman Catholic Church over-
came its earlier fears of syncretism and relativism and finally entered the ecumenical movement. Since the beginning of the sixties
the interpenetration of thought and the collaboration of scholars,
pioneers willing to experiment (and even a number of Church
leaders) have changed the ecclesiastical scene. Only coming gen-
erations will be able to see properly the revolutionary changes
that have taken place in the last decade.

There is no space in this article to analyse the origins of this
change in detail. We all know the most important components:
the decline of the Church's influence in political and social life,
with its related and hopeful theological discovery of the serving
Church; the emancipation of peoples and persons, resulting in a
great variety of expression and conviction; the rapid development
of industrial society into a cybernetic society with its threat of
scientific determinism; the slow but solid developments of
the historical sciences and their influence on the authority of

[4] Neill and Rouse, op. cit., chap. 17.

Scripture and tradition; the change from a rather static to a socially mobile society in which belonging to one well-defined community is the fate (or chance) of only a small minority. The list can easily be lengthened.

The Church in the midst of this change, resisting it through its institutions but promoting it at the same time through its proclamation, has changed considerably. The literature of the last ten to fifteen years testifies to this change. The ecumenical movement is both a result of and a reaction to it. It represents the need of Christians to stay close together, encouraging and comforting each other, as well as the liberation of Christian men and women from shackles, obstacles and beliefs which we now discover to be quite alien and often detrimental to the heart of the Christian faith.

But we have also discovered that the obstacles are formidable, especially those which are the products of fear and defensiveness. The reader of much of the so-called renewal theology of the last years, of the protest literature in the Christian community, must keep that perspective in mind. The discovery of the Church as a servant to the world, which is a community of availability and pro-existence, is made in an institutional framework in which authoritarianism, excessive wealth, complacency and collective egotism are still forming the outline of our communities the outsider sees. No stranger in Jerusalem sees a servant-community when he looks at the Christian Church: he sees a rich, defensive, arrogant ideological structure, within which a small group of leaders and simple followers have apparently seen a new light for which they pay heavily within their own ranks. No wonder that many of them are full of bitterness and speak in a tone which does not really belong in the Christian community. Until we have found institutions which encourage rather than suppress our freedom, a good number of the best people we have will remain doubtful about all institutions. If a number of people already speak of a post-ecumenical age, I hear and read in their contributions more of a plea for freedom and genuine ecumenicity than a solid attack on what happens in the ecumenical movement. During the Assembly of the WCC at Uppsala, it was noted by almost all present that all criticism of the Assembly was directed towards its structures, its representativeness and its working methods. On the content of the agenda there was no disagreement.

II. THEOLOGICAL STEWARDSHIP

One of the confusing elements today is provided by the inherent debate between a traditional theology which wants to define and limit and an ecumenical theology which is teleological, that is, which sets a goal for the Churches. A Church which has recognized itself to be *in via* will necessarily concentrate more on the future than on the past. While in Scripture past and future are reconciled in God's faithfulness, in our time we have trouble to reconcile our own witness to God's acts in our traditions and his invitation to his coming Kingdom.

Within this situation the last years have seen a new emphasis on common service of the Churches to the world. No wonder: a loss of political power coincided with a theological victory for those who, after centuries of a minority position, advocated that the true posture of the Church in the world is diaconal. Then there was the nineteenth-century experience of the extraordinary healing power of service in conflict. In the twentieth century this experience of the unifying quality of service coincided with the conceptual crisis of the Christian faith. In simple language: common service grew stronger, doctrinal certainty weaker. In 1925, at the first world conference for "Life and Work", this led to the naïve expectation that a common activity in social and political affairs could take the place of doctrinal agreement. Now after forty years of theological ecumenicity we know that it is not that simple. We have learned that common life, common study, common service, common witness and common prayer interpenetrate in such a way that not only does a new climate of relationships assert itself, but also theological ecumenicity changes into an ecumenical way of doing theology. Rather than the former explicative theology we grow into a posture of common theological questioning. Theology, without losing its identity or its unique contribution, loses its assumed independence. Instead of the magisterial proclamation of truths, it becomes the companion of all other searches for reliable truth. In an age in which scientists, politicians and economic leaders have to deal with new questions,

all pertaining to the basic elements of our societies and person-
alities, theology also dons its professorial gown and becomes a servant, participating in the debate, more often raising questions
than giving answers.

This is not a simple change. In WCC circles there is always a
complaint that the theologians seem to have lost their nerve. Both
at the World Conference on Church and Society 1966, and at the
Fourth Assembly, theologians were active participants but they
did not dominate the conferences. The older generation may get
nervous about this; an increasing number of Christians greet this
new humility with enthusiasm. Theological ecumenicity is in the
midst of finding a new role; the last traces of comparative theology are fading away. What is now needed is wise theological
stewardship which, from a deep knowledge of the tradition, con-
tributes what is effective and useful in the actual debates of mankind, in the world and in that part of the world that is the
Church. What has really happened is that theological ecumenicity
has lost its separateness. And that can only be an advantage.
Within this theological adventure many blind alleys are discovered. Some attempts to reformulate the truths of the Gospel
are quickly recognized as useless, or as interesting but inadequate
paths. They tend to be recognized as such pretty soon.[5] Others
however seem profitable and help our generation to witness with
intellectual integrity to the always remaining mysteries of faith.[6]

III. Specific Approach

What happens in all this to the confessional moments in
theology? Let us immediately state that they are certainly not
dead. Most of the confessional systems of conceptualizing the
Christian faith are too fundamental and alive to die easily. In the
great theological debates of our day they still play an important
role. For confessions are not only doctrinal agreements, rejections
of heresy or defensive documents of churchly identity, they are

---

[5] E.g., the debate on the Death of God theology. See Kenneth Hamilton,
God is Dead, the Anatomy of a Slogan (Grand Rapids, 1966). Id., Revolt
against Heaven (1968), and literature in both books.

[6] For example, the theology of hope, so ably begun by J. Moltmann,
Theology of Hope (London and New York, 1967).

vital expressions of the actual life of the community. They are results of the way in which a community relates to the history of a nation and its culture. They are the basis of the community's worship and the way in which it has traditionally understood history. So they have become an expression of ethos, directing a denomination in its witness to the surrounding human society. As such they are still responsible for such clearly recognizable directions as a confessing community takes today.

Each confessional family, therefore, shows a specific approach to the questions of our day. It is no wonder that the Reformed tradition seems to be most vocal in the theological debate on the transformation of society. It is no miracle either that the Lutheran concept of the two realms is a recurring theme. In Roman Catholic and Anglican theology, natural theology is still developing and is constantly reformulated so as to suit present needs. What is new and hopeful today is that confession and denomination can no longer be equated. We all know that the new threats of division and the new elements of unity cross all denominational boundaries. But confessional theology does too. An increasing number of Catholics have discovered the elementary truth of the *ecclesia semper reformanda*. An increasing number of theologians in the tradition of the Reformation move towards an episcopal understanding of ministry. Collegiality and the stress on the interdependence of almost independent local and national Churches are no longer contributions peculiar to the Congregationalist tradition. This is not to deny the vital contribution of the traditional confessions but to see them in their new context, confusing for some, liberating for others. But if the ecumenical movement had not at least produced this new situation, it would have failed miserably.

In all our denominations isolation belongs to the past and with that uniformity has had its day. The time in which we live is one of transition. That is as true for the Church as for society at large. We are moving into a period of pluralism in which inherited concepts and values become the property of all. This requires a new discipline of community life of which we have as yet little experience. Some people would like to proclaim that we already have attained this pluralist society and this plural community of faith. But here again we should be careful not to generalize too quickly. The many elements of pluralism may be all around and within us, but they have not yet been assimilated. The contestation in our universities, the fierce struggles for economic independence in the developing countries and last but not least the critical movements in the Churches testify to that. At the same time, and we might well underline this, the great majority of these movements are based on a deep loyalty to the contested institutions. That in itself identifies our time as a time of transition in which a momentous struggle goes on for the proper structures of our human enterprise.

IV. Accept the Truth of Others

We are living then at a time when divisive confessions become the property of all and play their own new role. That involves of course a reciprocal movement of correction in the whole of the Church. It is no longer possible, as indeed it never should have been, to regard a Christian confession as the unique property of one confessional family. A confession by its very nature seeks to engage the whole of the Church. Now a new debate emerges in which "outsiders" take serious issue with "our" confessions. Such debates are necessarily emotional because they touch the very foundations of our communities. In the ecumenical movement the real struggle for truth begins when we move from the first stage of comparison via the second stage of mutual, partial appreciation into the third stage of an attempt at appropriation in which we begin to accept the truth of others for ourselves.

This latter stage we have now entered. It is the stage in which the newly emerging community forges its own confessions. It is also the stage in which we move from dialogue between divided partners into fellowship, which means the dialogue within the one ecumenical movement. This pregnant expression of the one ecumenical movement, coined by the Joint Working Group of the Roman Catholic Church and the World Council of Churches,[7] indicates that the ecumenical movement is already more than a place of encounter. It is the most real expression of unity we have.

[7] See Second Report of the Joint Working Group in the *Ecumenical Review* (October 1967).

Of course this unity is still very imperfect and dangerously tentative but it is the movement towards full *"sumpnoia"*, to use a word of Basil the Great.[8] The new measure of unity we have found is imperfect, but so was our confessional unity. In both cases our unity is partial. Therefore the Churches are driven for the sake of their own confessional truth into a wider fellowship, in which they have to come to grips with their conflicting confessional loyalties.

How can that be done? Two methods are tried today. The first one requires absolute loyalty to the confessions of the historical community: a dangerous requirement. It pushes many to almost unacceptable callisthenics in the process of re-interpreting the confession in such a way that they can live with it. Others are willing to live in schizophrenia, praying for better times to come. Still others give up and leave. The other method is a consequent elaboration of the concept of the hierarchy of truths,[9] in which the central elements of the Christian faith are the common basis on which the debate about the others is carried on. It seems to me that most theologians today have accepted this and only disagree on the format of the common basis: some put more in there than others. Let us remember that in the Eastern tradition, theology was always defended as a free discipline on the basis of acceptance of the first ecumenical councils of the Church. In the *koinonia* of the WCC, the basic formula has played a comparable role;[10]

[8] Dr Eugene Carson Blake used these words in his welcoming address to Pope Paul in Geneva, June 1969: "We are bold to describe our fellowship with a word used by that great and sainted teacher of the East, Basil the Great, *'Sumpnoia'*, 'being together in one spirit'. This may sound almost presumptuous in the light of our failures to overcome our differences, to heal our divisions or even fully to understand the truth of the Gospel. Yet our experience of the presence of Christ in new and unexpected ways has brought us together in one spirit. Here, through mutual encouragement and mutual correction, we are finding new ways of living under his Lordship."

[9] Cf. *De Oecumenismo*, art. 11.

[10] The basic formula of the World Council of Churches reads as follows: "The World Council of Churches is a fellowship of Churches which confess the Lord Jesus Christ as God and Saviour according to the Scriptures and therefore seek to fulfil together their common calling to the glory of the one God, Father, Son and Holy Spirit."

There are people who feel that the unity formula of New Delhi should be added to understand the aim of the basis. Both formulas have confessional overtones without being confessions of faith in the formal sense of

the very fact of accepting a basis requires the concept of a hierarchy of truths. There is historical evidence that it also makes for
a dynamic concept of unity. Without it, all we can do is prepare
for a great future event in which suddenly the walls between the
confessional communities come tumbling down. This does not
seem a very likely prospect. It does not even seem a very desirable
prospect: unity does not come about by explosion or surrender:
it is a growth process on the basis of interior conversion.

Confessional differences in the Churches' relation to the rest of
the world can be a positive factor in the life of the whole people
of God. They demonstrate the diversity of possible expressions of
the one mystery of God's dealings with man. If the legitimacy of
this diversity is recognized, we can begin to reconsider their complementariness. This complementariness can only be reached in
dialogue, that is in serious consideration of the merits and the
errors of historical expressions of the Christian faith. Will that
be a long process or shall we discover that once we restore the
basic elements of the fellowship a number of reciprocal historical
condemnations simply lose their power and become obsolete? It
seems to me that the last ten years have clearly demonstrated the
latter development.

Many confessional differences have a rather simple explanation:
they were the results of the struggle of a particular Christian
community in a particular historical moment and a particular situation. Understood in their original context, they lose their
exclusive and perhaps even sectarian character. The confessional
documents of the time of the Reformation are also protest documents. For that part of them they are determined by the phenomena they protested against. When these phenomena change the

---

the word. The New Delhi formula reads: "We believe that the unity
which is both God's will and his gift to his Church is being made visible
as all in each place who are baptized into Jesus Christ and confess him
as Lord and Saviour are brought by the Holy Spirit into one fully committed fellowship, holding the one apostolic faith, preaching the one
Gospel, breaking the one bread, joining in common prayer, and having a
corporate life reaching out in witness and service to all and who at the
same time are united with the whole Christian fellowship in all places and
all ages in such wise that ministry and members are accepted by all, and
that all can act and speak together as occasion requires for the tasks to
which God calls his people."

protest loses its sting. But not its life: it has to be reformulated in order to continue its service as a warning, a reminder and an acceptable expression of faith. Its deepest intention, which is always its expression of loyalty to the apostolic faith *in toto*, has to be kept alive in the collective memory of the restored fellowship.

Whether confessional differences are enriching or divisive depends therefore on the quality of fellowship. If no steps towards fellowship are taken, the conflict between the confessions cannot be translated into tension and they remain negative. If the fellowship is being restored, positive tension replaces the destructive conflict.

Jos Lescrauwaet

Confessional Aspects in Contemporary Theology
4. Confessing the Faith in the Liturgy

ONE can trace the historical development of Western Christianity by following the problems connected with the confession of the Christian faith. By "confession" we mean here mainly the exclusively intellectual formulation of our Christian conviction, particularly as shaped by dogmatic theology. The fact that we can use the word in this way, and so can use it also in the plural —something we cannot do with "faith"—is already typical of the way in which the Westerner practises his faith. We treat the faith as if it exists in a kind of separate compartment in our experience. And so the schism between East and West was afterwards usually justified on the basis of dogmatic differences, while in the West every new breakaway led to a new confession.

The ecumenical dialogue dawdles along in the *"Konfessionskunde"* (the discussion of confession, or creed), and time and again it is dogma which constitutes the breaking-point. Even within each Church we are only too well aware of conflicts created by the "true" confession between orthodox and liberals, conservatives and progressives, fundamentalists and existentialists. The confessions of the last five centuries were mainly aimed at protecting the faith against errors, outside and within the Churches. Textbooks of those days were full of theological controversy, and catechisms concentrated on a doctrinal introduction to the Christian life, with the main emphasis often on apologetics.

Today we realize that our rational formulations of the faith have landed us in a difficult situation, within our own Church and the family of Churches, as well as in our relations with modern society. For some light on the problem we naturally turn to the way in which we started to confess our faith at the beginning.

I. Confessing God and Praising God

There is a very good reason why the New Testament word *"homologein"*, and its Vulgate equivalent *"confiteri"*, should refer to confessing the faith, confessing sin and praising God.[1]

In the New Testament several confessions of the faith take the form of a hymn (Eph. 1. 3–14; Phil. 2. 6–11; Col. 1. 15–20). The oldest confessions of the Church had their origin in the baptismal liturgy, and by the fifth century our own creed, composed to confute the Arian heresy, was already incorporated in the celebration of the Eucharist in the East. The Council of Toledo (589), which introduced the creed into the celebration of the Eucharist in the West, explained the reason for this: "That the hearts of Christians should be cleansed by the faith when they come forward to receive the body and blood of Christ."[2]

When celebrating the liturgy, the Church contemplates and listens to God's active presence among men, and in doing so becomes "Church" in the true sense of the word. She confesses the historical deeds and words of salvation in the threefold sense of "confessing" mentioned above: she expresses her faith, her sinfulness and her praise of God. It is then that the Church becomes the communal response to the Word that gathers men together, and so is then most herself, with a clear identity.

From the beginning this communion in faith was expressed in word and sacrament. The constant repetition of the liturgical celebration actualizes the Church's faith and confirms her in her existence as "the community of the faithful".

The liturgy is therefore the focal point where the Christ-event

---

[1] Cf. O. Michel in *ThWNT*, V, pp. 206 f.; the Old Testament *jadah* has the same complex meaning, see Köhler and Baumgartner, *Lexicon in Veteris Testamenti Libros* (Leiden, 1948), p. 363.

[2] Mansi, IX, c. 993. The East introduced the creed into every celebration of the Eucharist, which was also the intention of the decree of Toledo and, shortly after 798, that of Aix-la-Chapelle. The same probably holds for the Roman decree of 1014, but this was not insisted upon.

is handed on from one generation to another "until the Lord comes" (1 Cor. 11. 26). The "teaching of the apostles" was transmitted in faithfulness "to the brotherhood, to the breaking of the bread and to prayers" (cf. Acts 2. 42). The liturgy was as it were the continuum where the Word was understood in the context of praise, and where it was put into concrete practice through sacramental sharing. There God's self-communication in the Church becomes a living experience and this experience is an essential aspect of the Church's tradition.[3]

This is why the early Church, particularly in the East, spoke about worship as "primary theology" (*theologia prima*), while the dogmatic exploration of it all was called "secondary theology" (*theologia secunda*). Thus the word "orthodoxy" still always means primarily authentic praise, and only secondarily authentic doctrine.[4] That is why John Damascene called the eucharistic prayer "theology", and G. Florovsky still speaks of the Eucharist as "the witness in worship to the truth of the revelation".[5]

Here a confessional formula obviously plays a part, but it does so only as one moment in a complex experience. This rational formulation is put in the context of Christ's own, actual speaking to his faithful and his sacramental acting with them.

Christ's word is addressed to the whole man, that is, man in his actual situation at that moment. It demands a response, and is an enabling invitation to this response, so that communion is brought about, and, with it, community. In Augustine's striking terminology, Christ's word is an "audible sacrament".

This word is also put into practice by both Christ and his faithful in his sacrament, as in a "visible word"[6]—the communication of the faith through gestures.

The liturgical confession says that Jesus truly died and was raised up, but says it in response to him who now lives. In doing so the liturgical confession bears witness to this true fact among

[3] Cf. M. Thurian, *Amour et Vérité se rencontrent* (1956).
[4] Cf. R. Stählin, "Die Geschichte des christlichen Gottesdienstes", in *Leitourgia—Handbuch des evangelischen Gottesdienstes*, ed. by K. F. Müller and W. Blankenburg (Kassel, 1954), vol. I, p. 29.
[5] *Ways of Worship. The Report of a Theological Commission of Faith and Order*, ed. by P. Edwall, E. Hayman and W. D. Maxwell (London, 1951), p. 53.
[6] *Contra Faustum*, I. 19, ch. 16: *P.L.*, 42, 356-7.

those who share this faith. The liturgy expresses this as thanks-giving for and assent to (*homologeia*) that communication of Christ which says that "he was put to death for *our* sins and raised to life to justify *us*" (Rom. 4. 25).

This breaks through the mere formulation and penetrates into the personal reality which is greater and deeper than words can ever convey. In baptism this same article is pronounced and the baptized person joins in this death and resurrection of the Lord in a way which must pervade all his further life. Similarly, the paschal mystery is proclaimed in such a way to the baptized Christian that he can constantly make it actual in himself.

The separated Christian Churches live by this same mystery while quarrelling with each other about grace coming through faith or justification through baptism or communion with Christ and in Christ through the Lord's Supper. They recognize each other in their celebrations, and this the more readily as they stay closer to the biblical terminology and the original biblical ritual. A good example of this can be found in the conciliar decree on ecumenism where the reformed interpretation of the Eucharist is not countered with dogmatic quotations from the Council of Trent nor with references to some reformed confessional docu-ment, but only their liturgical intent is given.[7]

II. The Liturgical Confession of the Living God

One confessional crisis which today concerns all Christians, even those who manage to preserve the peace of faith in their own heart, concerns the Christian witness that God is a living God and that our world is not left to itself. The original Chris-tian witness to "the only true God, and Jesus Christ whom you have sent" (John 17. 3) is called into question. While there is no shortage of popular theological publications and public discus-sion, even born Christians begin to hesitate. This is why many rightly look to the Church and, like Augustine, say to themselves: "I would not believe the gospel if the Church's authority did not move me."[8] We need a confessing Church, a "community of the faithful" (the oldest description of the Church), that does

---

[7] *Unitatis redintegratio*, n. 22.
[8] *Contra epistolam Manichaei*, 1. 1, ch. 5: *P.L.*, 42, 177.

not merely offer us an intellectual formula but also practises to the full what she confesses, and communicates it in this practice.

The very existence of the Church is being questioned. There is doubt about her existence as the historical embodiment of Christ's witness to God in this world. The Church must constantly show the credibility of this fact in the original way in which she is the Church of Christ.

"Original" here does not mean merely "in accordance with the form the Church had at her origin in the days of the New Testament"; the word also implies that the Church must reflect her continuous re-birth in the Christian experience of Christ's word and sacrament.

The liturgical assembly is not a merely traditional, conventional and useful—but for the rest incidental—circumstance of Christian life. It is the essential and permanently original experience and manifestation of it. Here the word which creates the Church is unceasingly proclaimed and received in faith. Here Christ's life-giving activity is accomplished through faithful participation in it. Here Christ's self-communication is always *in origine*—at the root. And so the way is opened here towards the God who lives and does not leave the world to itself.

In this worship the Church is able to speak about the reality of God without doubt and without presumption, without hesitation and without pretentiousness. "Driven by a spontaneous necessity, born of the Spirit, the Church simply states in the creed what *is*. She does not ask why she does it, nor for what purpose, nor with what result. She simply *has* to do it because God's reality has overpowered her."[9]

The liturgical confession does not prove God, but witnesses to his reality as to a mystery which neither needs nor tolerates an explicit defence. It does not analyse God's existence but approaches it constantly from another angle.

The liturgy makes us live the mystery of our own existence as both a questioning reference and an assenting response to the

[9] P. Brunner, "Zur Lehre vom Gottesdienst", in *Leitourgia*, etc., p. 259. Cf. J. Lescrauwaet, "Liturgie en hedendaags levensbesef", in *Geloof bij kenterend getij*, ed. by H. Fiolet and H. van der Linde (Roermond, ²1968), pp. 294–6.

mystery of God. This experience, which is not merely intellectual but embraces the whole man, not merely individual but communal, is not a victory over the sacred but a contact with it. And to this contact the Christian community bears witness in the way Jesus did, who is both man and God's Christ.

The community bears witness to this reality, first of all, by being Church, and explicitly the Church of him whose life comes from and goes towards the Father. Word and sacrament must again fulfil their most original function, which is to establish the means of communication which create and confirm the community, and through which the Lord builds himself a body in the world and in history (see 1 Cor. 12. 12–27 and Eph. 4. 1–16). This self-communication of Jesus Christ constitutes a fully human communion with himself as *the* Son, who operates as "the eldest of many brothers" (Rom. 8. 29).

The communion between Christ and the faithful implies the mutual sharing of spiritual and material wealth among his faithful. Both the reality of Christ and the reality of his Father are actually brought close to us in this sacramental and social communion. Today we are badly in need of this sacramental and social communion to enable us to live in our world in faith, hope and sharing.

This evangelical confession assures us of a meaningful existence and is the ground of our hope and joy (cf. Heb. 11. 1 and Rom. 12. 12). This faith and this hope are given us as a community. God gives them to us when we share them with each other in his name.

The words and sacraments of the faith are Christ's but they do not fall out of the sky. Since the incarnation of the Son and the outpouring of the Spirit of the Son (Gal. 4. 6) these words and sacraments circulate among the faithful. In this communion, this "we", Christ is actively present, witnesses to the reality of God and thus gathers us together.

The confession is therefore the liturgical assembly itself with all that this community does in the social life of every day. The authentic liturgy with its social implications is the most intelligible and credible confession of the existence of a God who is "communion".

III. The Liturgical Confession as Peace within the Church

Christians meet regularly to share their one faith in the confession of God, to elucidate it among themselves and to encourage each other to put it into practice. They meet to confess together their common trust in the Lord and thus to confirm each other. They are together in order to witness to God's love of man, to recognize this love both with each other and in each other.

In this worship there is therefore room for those who incline to a predominantly objective confession which clearly interprets the events and words of salvation history, and for those who prefer the subjective aspect which stresses the personal surrender to the ineffable Mystery.[10] The liturgical way of confessing makes it possible for both tendencies to be at ease.

Because both types of faithful tend to project their preferences on matters of dogma and theological opinion, both types experience a sense of malaise with regard to the confessional Church. One group is afraid that the Church betrays her nature because she allows all kinds of subjective interpretations of the encounter with God in the Church of Christ, interpretations strongly influenced by the modern mentality. The other fears that the Church is losing her identity because of her rigid clinging to a mentality and images that are now a thing of the past. This leads only too easily to the use of labels such as modernism or fundamentalism, subjectivism or denominationalism, liberalism or dogmatism. To a large extent these differences can be reduced in liturgical theology to differences that arise within one confession.

On the other hand, liturgical theology is not merely the expression of religious self-awareness or momentary religious emotionalism. It has a definite subject-matter, it refers to events in salvation history and tries to express a basic answer to whatever reaches the faithful from God. The way the liturgy expresses this is moreover essentially communal, not only in the present but also in a deliberately maintained continuity with the believing community of all ages.

On the other hand, liturgical theology is not a way of denominational or supra-personal thinking. It is meant to serve the

[10] Cf. E. Griese, *Perspektiven einer liturgischen Theologie* (*Una Sancta*, 24, 1969), pp. 102–4.

actual and personal practice of the faith. It is a kind of existential anamnesis. It deals with the active and sacramental confession of faithful who live in their own actual situation.

The Christian faith is the response to the Word, that not only spoke but became truly man and shared in the full human reality. This Word sheds light on the mystery of our whole human existence by referring it to the mystery of him to whom all existence must return.

The reaction of our confession to the revelations of the mystery of God's presence leads as much to wonder as to reflection. It expresses itself as much in silence as in verbal witness. It understands by intuition as much as through analysis. And finally, it finds itself in the acceptance of facts as much as in the surrender to him whom we encounter in those facts.

Thus the confessional moments in the liturgy offer a variety of confessional possibilities. Since the liturgy is the "original" *locus* of confession for the community, these various possibilities are justified. The communal celebration of word and sacrament is the true moment of reconciliation.

Translated by Theo Westow

Gustave Thils

From Ecumenism to Ecumenicity

I. ECUMENISM

THE term "ecumenism" first gained acceptance in Catholic circles about thirty years ago, thanks to Yves Congar's outstanding work, *Chrétiens désunis. Principes d'un oecuménisme catholique* (Eng. trans., *Divided Christendom. A Catholic Study of the Problems of Reunion*, London, 1939). Nevertheless, the word still had a Protestant flavour about it, as far as many Catholics of the time were concerned. In rather the same way *Dogmengeschichte* began by being a purely Protestant theological discipline whereas now the history of dogma is studied everywhere.

The French name for the World Council of Churches uses the adjective "ecumenical": *Conseil oecuménique des Eglises*, as does the German: *Oekumenischer Rat der Kirchen*, whereas the Greeks prefer *Koinonia ton Ekklesion* (Amsterdam, 30 August 1948). The word "ecumenical" has always had its supporters among the pioneers of the modern ecumenical movement. During the preparations for the World Missionary Conference in Edinburgh (1910), some people suggested it should be called the Ecumenical Missionary Conference, a proposal which was not accepted on the grounds that "ecumenical" had a technical meaning. And in 1919 Archbishop Söderblom called for an Ecumenical Council of Churches, but it was felt that there were certain disadvantages in using those words. The term was adopted in 1948 for the title *Conseil oecuménique des Eglises* because, in spite of the already lengthy history of the word, it possessed a certain amount of flexibility, evoked the supra-racial, supra-national and universal character of the Church, and was well suited to express the new approach to the question of restoring unity between the different Churches.[1]

That is the principal purpose of the World Council of Churches: to be a "brotherly association of Churches" unfortunately cut off from one another, and to be a new prophetic instrument for the restoration of the one, holy Church, according to God's plan. Both within the movement and outside it, all eyes are fixed on the 160 member Churches (1948), and a common prayer is offered to the Lord bidding him hasten the day when they will be the one Church of God. That was, and still is, the meaning given to the word "ecumenism".

This desire is valid and its object a matter of urgency. And yet, on the whole, it scarcely interests the younger generation. Why?

To some extent the lack of interest in inter-Church affairs is to be explained by the slowness of the process of restoring unity. How can one enthuse, for example, about the *rapprochement* between Roman Catholics and Orthodox when one notices that these two Churches have taken so long to make a move towards one another, even though they are already extremely close in basic dogma and the essential requirements for unity? Older people, whose knowledge of Church history has taught them to be patient, regret the considerable influence of non-dogmatic factors and await better days. The young, who tend rather to be scandalized by their acquaintance with the history of the Churches, lose interest and follow paths less encumbered with innumerable obstacles of so many shapes and sizes. Do we not get the same impression when we study the history of the World Council of Churches? Having begun with 160 member Churches in 1948, today, in spite of its endless work—and notwithstanding the fact that certain Churches of a "Protestant" tendency require a less detailed dogmatic conformity than Churches of the "Catholic" type—it numbers 232 Churches with full or associate membership.

The decline in interest is also to be explained by the kind of civilization in which we live. Our contemporaries react much

[1] On all this see W. A. Visser 't Hooft, *The Meaning of Ecumenical* (London, 1953), pp. 22–7.

more readily to universal human problems, such as peace and economic development. Consequently Church or inter-Church affairs rapidly and inevitably assume a "sectarian" air. Already during the Second Vatican Council various bishops from Africa and Asia alluded in their speeches to the need for a wider ecumenism than that with which the Churches are concerned: in fact they had in mind an irenic approach and a dialogue between the Church and the different religions and traditions of the world. But there is more to it than this; a wider view is needed.

II. Towards Ecumenicity

From the very beginnings of the ecumenical movement, ecumenism in practice as well as the word itself had wider implications which sooner or later were bound to shatter more limited conceptions of it. In fact the International Missionary Council was involved from the start; it helped to organize world-wide conferences, kept in close touch with the ecumenical bodies, became more and more integrated, and finally joined forces with the World Council of Churches. Its whole inner momentum has been in the direction of turning the attention of Church leaders away from their frequent obsession with internal problems towards, so to speak, the "ends of the earth".

In a similar way the movement known as Life and Work—through its ceaseless activity "in the world", its initiatives in the struggle for peace and in the sphere of social problems, education, development and so on—regularly reminded the representatives of the Churches that they should be "open to the world", and prevented them from becoming too exclusively absorbed in their internal problems, however real and important these might be.

Moreover, the term "ecumenical" and the idea of "ecumenicity", because they suggest so much, sometimes led people to go beyond what is normally and rightly understood by "ecumenism", namely "a movement for the restoration of unity between the separated Christian Churches". The leaders of the movement were led to question "the meaning of ecumenical". Ecumenists asked themselves the same question, more theoretically perhaps, but none the less instructively.[2] Their researches produced some

[2] See M. Prisilla, "Oekumenisch", in *Stimmen d. Zeit*, 119 (1930),

fundamental studies of *oikumene*[3] either in a secular[4] or a biblical[5] context. Christian antiquity also made frequent use of the word and attributed a bewildering complexity of meaning to it: universality, catholicity, wholeness, unity, doctrinal orthodoxy, all rolled into one indefinable concept, with varying geographical, cultural or political emphases.[6] But all these studies of the meaning of ecumenism had one thing in common: they revealed an idea of *oikumene* extending beyond, and sometimes well beyond, the scope of "the problem of the reunion of the Christian Churches".

In the inspired Scriptures, *oikumene* means first of all the whole world, the whole of mankind in so far as it has received everything from its Creator and belongs wholly to him. The history of salvation takes place in the world and in mankind. *Oikumene* is even mankind caught up in the economy of salvation of Christ Jesus, as in Hebrews 2. 5: *oikumene mellousa* is mankind in the messianic era which began with the Lord Jesus.[7] There can therefore be an ecumenical movement built on the notion of ecumenicity in its most complete theological sense.

At the meeting of the *Comité Central de Paris* (1962), Visser 't Hooft made a speech which, if not a turning-point, can certainly be considered a sign-post and an important moment in the

---

pp. 257–70; E. Fascher, "Oekumenisch und Katholisch", in *Theol. Literaturz.*, No. 85 (1960), pp. 7–20; H. van der Linde, *Wat is oekumenisch?* (Roermond-Maaseik, 1961), 34 pp.

[3] For an overall study, see Pauly-Wissowa's *Realenzyclopädie der klassischen Altertumwissenschaft*, vol. XVII, 2, "Oikumene", pp. 2123–2174.

[4] J. Kaerst, *Die antike Idee der Oikumene in ihrer politischen und kulturellen Bedeutung* (Leipzig, 1903) (Hellenistic world, culture); J. Vogt, *Orbis Romanus, Zur Terminologie der Römanischen Imperialismus* (Tübingen, 1929), 32 pp. (Roman world, juridical order).

[5] For the New Testament: O. Michel, "Oikumene", in *Theol. Wörterb. z. Neuen Test.*, vol. V, pp. 159–61; further reading: M. Paeslack, "Die 'oikumene' im Neuen Testament", in *Theologia Viatorum*, 2 (1950), pp. 33–47.

[6] Two works which bring out this complexity: A. Tuilier, "Le sens de l'adjectif 'oecuménique' dans la tradition patristique et dans la tradition byzantine", in *Nouv. Rev. Théol.*, No. 86 (1964), pp. 260–71; P. H. Muraille, "L'Eglise, peuple de l'Oikuménè d'après saint Grégoire de Naziance", in *Ephem. Theol. Lovanien*, No. 44 (1968), pp. 154–78.

[7] Cf. G. Thils, *Histoire doctrinale du mouvement oecuménique* (Louvain, [2]1963), pp. 223–4.

history of the movement. The end of his speech was devoted to an examination of the meaning of *oikumene*. Our ecclesiastical tasks, he said, were now so many that we were in danger of forgetting the world outside the Church. It would seem that just to get to know each other, to enter into a real theological conversation with each other and to co-operate in the task of renewal of the Church's life, was already as much as we could hope to accomplish in the coming years. But that was a temptation. "There can be no self-contained and introverted ecclesiastical *oikumene*. There can be only a Church *oikumene* which realizes that Christ is Lord and which must now carry that testimony in word and deed to the wider *oikumene* which does not yet recognize what God has done for and in the world. It is in our mission and service among men that we realize our ecumenical purpose. This is not to underestimate the importance of true unity."[8] This last point is noteworthy: mission and service, but without detracting from the role of the search for unity between the Churches. In other words, our sights are to be set on ecumenicity but without neglecting the proper aim of ecumenism. There we have a revealing change of emphasis.

III. ECUMENICITY TODAY

Ecumenicity has to do with the nature of the Church; it is a property, a mark of the Church—rather like catholicity; and it means at one and the same time universality, wholeness and integrity, as we can gather from the way the word was used by the Fathers of the Church. To promote ecumenicity is to co-operate in the multiform deployment of the Church's resources, in its growth in depth as much as in its world-wide expansion, in the continually renewed *aggiornamento* of its activity and image, as well as in its grounding in apostolic continuity. All this expresses the fundamental and permanent element in the ecumenicity of the Church.

Each different epoch naturally and necessarily emphasizes one or another aspect of the mystery of the Church. Our generation's ecumenical endeavours take on the character of the times, which

[8] Text from *The Ecumenical Review*, XV (1962–63), pp. 74–81; *Istina* (1963), pp. 205–10.

includes a high degree of collaboration with all men of good will, a prime concern for the people of God compared with the institution, and a secular approach. We must assess the consequences of this for the Church and for ecclesiology.

The Church finds its complete fulfilment in the kingdom of God. Biblical scholars try to tell us how, a little more exactly. But we are still in the intermediary phase—the "interim" period as St Augustine called it. We find that there are just men and sinners in the Churches: a fact which dogmatic teaching insists on. Outside the visible Churches there are men of good will who (the theologians assure us) are justified and live in the Spirit. There exists, therefore, partly within and partly outside the visible Churches, a community of men leading a life of fundamental moral rectitude (to use the language of the letter from the Holy Office to Mgr Cushing), a life led in and according to the Spirit, with the grace and gifts of the Spirit, even though some of them may know nothing about the Christian revelation. This community here below is in the truest sense the prelude, foundation and beginning of the community of the elect—the heavenly Jerusalem. This community lacks an organic structure, but it enjoys "spiritual" brotherhood and fellowship across the network of the religious and secular institutions and structures of this world. Those who belong to it "feel that they are friends and brothers to each other, at one in their hope and in their actions", whenever they meet. Many of our contemporaries are attracted by participation in such a community, which satisfies their deepest longings. Their satisfaction is frequently accompanied—especially in the case of those on the more active and, as it were, prophetic wing—by a diminished respect for the Churches, religions or parties, which of course always include, sometimes by definition, just men and sinners, ardent enthusiasts and the mediocre.

The Church is also the leaven, the "sacrament", at one and the same time the sign and the means of intimate union with God and of the unity of all mankind (*Lumen gentium*, n. 1) or, as the penultimate draft of the Constitution put it very well: "The Church is both sign and instrument, as the sacrament of the profound unity of the whole human race and of its union with God." A "restricted" community is the sacrament of unity, salvation and happiness for the human community "at large". But here one can stress on one or other pole. Some emphasize the importance and concern for the restricted community, alleging that if it is well governed and highly united, it must be the leaven it is expected to be. But many Christians today consider that the restricted community—the Church, the Churches—is too engrossed in its own problems and ecclesiastical differences. They prefer to emphasize concern for, and the development of, the wider community, the human *oikumene*, in order to bring about brotherhood, peace, justice and human betterment—in short, the fruits of the Holy Spirit. And is that not the *res* of which the Church is the *sacramentum*? Moreover, "these values of human dignity, brotherhood and freedom, and the good fruits of our nature and enterprise, which we have nurtured on earth in obedience to the Lord and in his Spirit", do not belong only to "this" world: "we will find them again, but freed from stain, burnished and transformed" (*Gaudium et spes*, n. 39). Ecclesial ecumenicity in the spirit of *Gaudium et spes* is everywhere welcome. But, given this type of focus, interest in laboriously whittling down disputes between the Churches (in other words, in ecumenism) is apt to pale somewhat.

Another aspect of ecclesiology reveals an identical tendency. When one of the faithful lives according to his condition as an active member of the Christian community, he makes a mental distinction between the end, the means and the group of means involved. The end, at any rate here below, is the ever deeper and wider growth of the community of those who live in the Spirit, according to the Lord, and who enjoy the fruits of the Spirit in abundance: charity, justice, peace, purity and happiness. The means is the ensemble of activities corresponding to each individual's vocation. In concrete terms these activities are for the most part temporal or "secular". And those who take on and carry out these tasks are mostly those whom the Constitution *Lumen gentium* refers to as "the laity" (nn. 33. 34). Lastly, the group of means is the Church, in so far as it is the "general means of salvation" or bundle of numerous different "means of sanctification" offered to all the faithful in the name of the Lord; and these means are more or less closely bound up with the virtue of religion so that, in this respect, the Church is religious and a "religion".

What do we see happening today? Psychologically, in the case of many of the faithful, primacy is given to the end, the growth of the whole human community *in Spiritu*. Dare one reproach them for this? Then comes the means, the activity proper to each individual vocation, which is normally secular in kind. Is this reprehensible? Lastly, there is the "means of salvation", or the Church-as-the-means-of-salvation, which is put at the service of the ends and the means, and which will be respected in proportion to its true effectiveness and not on account of any nobility attached to the "sacred" in itself.

In all this the institutional Church does not take first place. But can a "means" to an end expect more than this? The element of secularity that inevitably goes with the realization of this type of "ecumenicity" does not prevent it from being authentically "spiritual", *in Spiritu* and therefore Christian; all that is necessary (and it is indeed necessary) is that the spirit of charity inspiring it should really be the *agape* of the New Testament. Nor does the subsidiary interest accorded the Church as the "means of salvation" prevent this type of ecumenicity from being profoundly religious; it is necessary and sufficient to preserve the theological dimension and to link it to the sacramental structure instituted by the Lord.

Conclusion

The ecumenical movement could explicitly adopt ecumenicity as an ideal, together with everything it entails. Catholics will applaud, because ecumenicity is an ecclesiological reality which is essential to the very mystery of the Church. The W.C.C., moreover, already has experience of it, thanks to the spirit inherited from the three movements: the International Missionary Council, Life and Work, and Faith and Order. Would the specific aim of ecumenism—the restoration of the unity which has been broken, be affected and impeded? Perhaps, but in appearance rather than in reality. For to put ecumenicity first and to promote it together or at least side by side with ecumenism is not only to give ecumenism wider scope on earth, but above all actually to inaugurate a life in communion (albeit imperfect) among Churches now on the way to full communion with each other. Even if it were to last as long as the Church itself, ecumenism is a movement for unity; ecumenicity is part and parcel of God's Church.

Translated by Jonathan Cavanagh

PART II
DOCUMENTATION
CONCILIUM

Concilium General Secretariat

Ecumenism in
Search of an Identity

THE foregoing articles in this issue show clearly enough that ecumenism is no longer a univocal concept. Nevertheless, the articles on ecumenism in recent reference works[1] still deal mainly with the external history of the institutionalization of the ecumenical movement.

Every movement usually has various foci. One focus of the ecumenical movement became institutionalized early on. It has been said that this too early institutionalization is already in danger of becoming hard-set in the shape of the World Council of Churches, with its centre at Geneva. But other foci of the ecumenical movement have not yet reached that degree of fixedness.

Articles in various periodicals usually extend the notion of ecumenism. The "ecumenical movement" refers then not only to various measures that may lead to the union of the many Christian denominations, but to the union of whole religions,[2] cultures

---

[1] The *Lexikon f. Theol. u. Kirche* (2nd edn., 1957–67), *Die Religion in Gesch. u. Gegenwart* (3rd edn., 1957–65), *Sacramentum Mundi* (1967 f.), and *A Dictionary of Christian Ethics* (96–99) devote only one long article to the ecumenical movement; the first two also have some more material in the articles "Ökumenik" and "Ökumenisch". Only *Sacramentum Mundi* deals with "ecumenical theology". An extensive bibliography on ecumenism may be found in H. Döring, *Kirchen unterwegs zur Einheit* (Munich, 1969), pp. 583–92; J. Lescrauwaet, *Compendium van het Oecumenisme* (Roermond, 1962) and *Einheit der Oekumene* (1969).

[2] The term was first used by E. Benz in *Zeitschr. f. Religions- u. Geistesgesch* (1951), p. 58; see H. Kraemer, "De oecumene der wereldreligies?", in *Oecumene in 't vizier* (Feestbundel voor Visser 't Hooft, Amsterdam, 1960), pp. 121–9. The reviews published by Aquinas University College,

and not infrequently even the whole world—which is felt to be the most urgent need, as expressed in the slogan "one world or none".

Yet there is a certain reluctance or fear attached to whatever purports to be ecumenism. This comes not only from the inevitable wear-and-tear that besets any movement that has already lasted for thirty years, but from various other causes as well.

I. THE MYTH OF THE ONE WORLD

A first cause lies in the conviction that the end of history is the creation of a single human community living in peaceful co-existence, a conviction seen as too optimistic, particularly by historians. For many it is not quite so obvious that this world is on the way towards a growing unity. Many see the historical process as we observe it today as a step towards self-destruction. Huizinga, the exponent of cultural philosophy, pointed to historical uncertainty when he refused to qualify the history of modern man as progress, and saw instead a progressive uncertainty whether the bridges in the paths we have chosen have not already been blown up, so that any aim we may have is henceforth beyond our reach.[3]

Even those who accept the unity and community of mankind as the *effective* aim of history wonder, nevertheless, whether we take man's historicity seriously enough when we speak of unity as the *normative* purpose of history. Historical awareness, which constitutes perhaps one of the most far-reaching developments in society today, prevents modern man from accepting the unity of mankind as something established *a priori*, and from seeing in the historical development of mankind simply a kind of

---

Colombo (Ceylon), *Quest* and *Logos*, show a definite tendency in this direction. Cf. T. Balasuriya, "Christian-Buddhist Dialogue in Ceylon", in *Logos*, 10 (1969/2), pp. 43–51; B. de Kretser, "Oecumenism in the One World", in *Quest.*, IV (1969/35 and 36), pp. 144 f. See also G. Baum, "'Les religions' dans la théologie catholique contemporaine: Vers une approche oecuménique", in *IDOC*, 5 (1 July 1969), pp. 75–93.

[3] Quoted in "Unité de l'Eglise—unité de l'humanité. Document d'étude de Foi et Constitution, Genève, Oct. 1969", in *IDOC*, 15 (1 Jan. 1970), p. 26.

illustration of this inevitable unity, already established at the creation of man.

He sees this unification as the result of an historical process the control of which is passing more and more into his own hands, and which he tries to bring about by the realization of limited and provisional objectives. Here sociology and economics seem more important to him than a firm belief in a pre-established unity which will ultimately be granted to man as a gift of God, and which divine providence finally manages to rescue from man's constant failures.

This vanishing conviction that the unity of mankind will have to arrive, come what may, also forces theology to re-examine the relationship between the kingdom of God and history on the one hand, and between the eschatological hope of the Christian and commitment to the provisional objectives of history on the other.[4]

It is therefore not astonishing in this situation that the Commission on Faith and Order discussed at its meeting of 1967 in Bristol what role the Church can play with regard to this divine plan to make this world one world.[5]

This also forced the Commission to discuss a question still more closely connected with the purpose of the World Council: What is the relationship between the attempt made by many Churches to achieve unity among themselves, and that hope of unity which lives in all mankind? The Commission published a provisional report on these questions in 1969.

Typically, the report contains more questions than answers. This is hardly astonishing, because consideration of this problem is rather recent in ecclesiastical circles. It starts from the sociological fact that today mankind is scientifically building up a kind of unity, by way of technology, economics and sociology. The question then arises how this scientific approach affects what

---

[4] This attempt has been made by the "theologians of revolution", such as Harvey Cox, J. B. Metz, J. Moltmann, R. Shaull and many others. Cf. T. Rendtorff and H. E. Tödt, *Theologie der Revolution. Analysen und Materialien* (Frankfurt a.M., 1968); H. Peukert (ed.), *Diskussion zur "politischen Theologie"* (Munich/Mainz, 1969); E. Feil and R. Weth (ed.), *Diskussion zur "Theologie der Revolution"* (Munich/Mainz, 1969), with ext. bibl.; and the November issue of *Wending*, 24 (1969), "Culturele revolutie".   [5] See note 3.

many Churches see as the aim of their ecumenical movement. This then prompts the Churches to find out how provisional their contribution to this process of unification is supposed to be.

The Churches can no longer see themselves as the centre of the whole world, around which that unification of the world has to take shape. If unity is to be achieved in this world it will be on the lines of a freedom ethically structured and acquired.

The Churches can contribute to this unification in so far as they can stimulate the process of liberation. Instead of being the centre round which this unity would, as if obviously, have to be built up, the Churches have become partners working together with many others who, with all the possible means provided by modern science, try to guide this historical process in the direction of unification. This is why, of the two trends that have existed in the World Council since the beginning, the movement of Life and Work is again becoming more prominent than that of Faith and Order.

The point is no longer to carry on the dialogue between theologians until they eventually produce some minimal creed, acceptable to all the member Churches. It is rather the Churches' mission to offer an effective service to the world in their common obedience to the one Lord.

W. A. Visser 't Hooft[6] considered this the first dynamic factor that could extricate the World Council from its present impasse:

> We must resume the dialogue with the world. . . . For a long time the Churches ignored or even condemned the world. When, in 1925, a Conference was held at Stockholm on Christianity in practice, Dr Patijn declared that the Church and the world had found each other again after centuries of pietism. . . . The Churches are trying to understand the world by listening to what it has to say; they ask themselves how they can continue their specific service in the new historical situation. It is curious that this basic change in the Churches' attitude towards the world has become an ecumenical fact. . . . On the one hand, we see in the Catholic Church an evolution which passed from the *Syllabus* of Pius IX, with its condemnation of the major ideas of the nineteenth century, to *Gaudium et Spes*, of Vatican II, which opened up the possibility

[6] In "Dynamic Factors in the Ecumenical Situation", in *The Ecumenical Review*, XXI (Oct. 1969), pp. 320–31.

of collaboration between the Church and the modern world. On the other hand, the evolution in the other Churches passed from the notions of Friedrich Julius Stahl in Germany, or Groen van Prinsterer in the Netherlands (who both saw in the history of their age the beginning of a period of unbelief and destructive revolutions), to the Conference on Church and Society, of 1966, and the Assembly of Uppsala, of 1968, where the Church's function with regard to development at world level occupied a key position.

This brief outline of the first reason why interest in ecumenism is on the decline already provides us with a pointer towards the new identity of the ecumenical movement. It can no longer be identified with one or several existing institutionalized forms of the ecumenical movement. It can no longer be seen as standing side by side with, or above the unification of the world. By the availability of its service it can, however, become an integral part of this historical process of unification if, with the help of its own means and resources, it can foster the community of a mankind that has become free.

II. Is there a Crisis within the Ecumenical Movement?

A second reason for the dwindling enthusiasm for ecumenism in the limited sense of the word might be put as follows: even if all Christian Churches could manage to achieve a recognizable unity among themselves, they would still bear the stigma of being merely a sect in this increasingly unified world.[7] This kind of perspective does not exactly encourage us to work for the actual unification of the Churches. A look at what is going on at present in this field already shows that the actual union of the Churches is going backward rather than forward.

When one looks at the various negotiations between the Churches to achieve union, one is faced repeatedly with incomprehensible failures. The negotiations between Anglicans and Methodists were rejected by the decisive meeting of the Anglicans.[8] The dialogue between Lutherans and Reformed Churches

[7] In his art. "Zur Soziologie kognitiver Minderheiten", in *Internationale Dialog Zeitschrift*, 2 (1969,²), pp. 127-32, Peter L. Berger describes the two possible Church models: the Church as sect or the Church largely adjusted to society.

[8] *One in Christ*, V (1969,⁴) contains a documentation on "Anglican-

in Europe seemed to be making good progress, yet the official reactions of the Lutheran Church have really reduced the results to nothing at all;[9] and the interim meeting of the World Council at Canterbury in 1969 was definitely disappointing.[10]

There are sound reasons for these failures. It is almost certain that many Anglo-Catholics rejected union with the Methodists because they worried about their position in their negotiations with the Catholics, and about a possible reinforcement of their Protestant wing. They must have thought that this would impair the question of Roman recognition of Anglican orders, which is pending.

There is also still the sociological undercurrent: the Church of England is even today the Church of the upper classes, whereas the Methodists represent the man-in-the-street. However, services of reconciliation and intercommunion are held in many places.

This makes the situation rather confused from the denominational angle, but in practice unity begins to assert itself.

This last point interests the younger generation in particular. They do not attach much importance to ecclesiastical discussion, because they are convinced that the prestige of the various Churches and the consolidation of their position exercise more influence here than the authorities are willing to admit.[11] Visser 't Hooft had great difficulty in Canterbury in getting a resolution through which would make sure that there would be fifteen to twenty members of under thirty present at the next session in 1971.[12]

Methodist Unity" (pp. 479–86), including the letter of the Archbishop of Canterbury and a Catholic commentary. The October number of *Theology*, LXXII (Oct. 1969) is wholly given up to the theme of "After the vote". See also *The Church Quarterly*, 2 (Oct. 1969), with several articles about the concept of function or office.

[9] Cf. "Das Memorandum des Lutherischen Einigungswerkes", in *Luth. Monatshefte*, 8 (1969/1), pp. 38 f.

[10] See the analysis in *Herder Korrespondenz*, 23 (1969/10), pp. 460–2, "Stagnation beim Weltrat der Kirchen" and F. König, "Ökumene in der Krise?", in *Luth. Monatshefte*, 8 (1969/10), pp. 485 f.; *Inf. cath. intern.* (Aug. 1969), n. 341–132, p. 10.

[11] Cf. *Herder Korrespondenz*, 23 (1969/8), pp. 354 f., "Nach dem Scheitern des Unionsplans zwischen Anglikanern und Methodisten". E. Timiadis mentions some interesting "Disregarded Causes of Disunity", in *The Ecumenical Review*, XXI (1969/4), pp. 299–309.

[12] See König's article (note 10 above).

It is therefore not surprising that people consider the ecumenism officially sanctioned by the Churches out of date. Statements about what has been called political Christianity[13] are only
addressed to the Western world. Not a word is said about anti-
Semitism in the East.

If the Churches really want to influence the unification process
that is taking place in contemporary history they cannot limit
themselves to a general rejection of racism, nuclear weapons,
war, and so on, but will have to tackle all structures—the ecclesiastical ones included—which foster these evils. At Canterbury[14]
this turning to the real facts of this world was still considered a
youthful indiscretion of ecumenism.

Then there is the well-known fact that the presence of the
Orthodox Churches has hampered the proceedings. There is also
the continued absence of the Catholic Church from the World
Council. On the other hand, a Catholic presence might hamper
the effectiveness of the World Council still more, certainly as
long as the social prestige of the individual Churches still plays
such a prominent part. In this context one can appreciate the
mutual reluctance which became evident on both sides when
Pope Paul visited Geneva.[15]

All this increases the difficulties of the Secretariat of the World
Council, since it has to execute the will of an assembly which
seems itself to have great difficulty in reaching any decisions at
all. Moreover, from the beginning, half a century ago, the World
Council has retained the character of a kind of society: it was
and still is something—in some cases even a hobby—for a few
who are directly interested, but not a concern of the mass of
people. So far the World Council has failed really to inspire and
actively stimulate the member Churches. It has not yet managed
to occupy the position and perform the function of a centre for
inter-Church communication. Far too many actual questions
about the faith seem to remain permanently locked up in the
office-desks of the various member Churches.

The same situation can be observed in the National Council of

---

[13] *Ibid.*   [14] *Ibid.*
[15] Cf. "Der Papstbesuch in Genf", in *Herder Korrespondenz*, 23 (1969/7),
pp. 301-3.

Churches[16] in the United States. Dissolution of the Council is already mooted by the Council itself. Powerfully institutionalized, it seems incapable of exercising any real influence on the member Churches. Black Power and the whole negro question are putting the Council in an untenable position, particularly now that a Black Theology is becoming increasingly articulate.[17] The Council is in favour of a progressive policy, but this policy is now being attacked by the negroes and the financially powerful Churches. The coloured masses rightly refuse to be integrated in what they call a "white" vision of the faith and a "white" theology; they are determined to establish first their own identity within their own culture.

On the other hand, the established Churches are too heavily conditioned by their past and too little concerned with the future. But to be realistically orientated towards the future of Christianity one needs a clear idea of aims; it will not do simply to maintain a *status quo,* however laudable it may be. A union of Churches without such an inspiring purpose for the future, as is the situation of the Churches in the United States, is bound to fail.

A more positive point made at the Canterbury assembly[18] was the idea, launched by Lukas Vischer, of a genuine general Council of all the Christian Churches. Here he took up an idea that was already suggested in Uppsala, especially by the younger participants. Such a general Council would then become an aim of the ecumenical movement. It would presuppose some already existing communion between the Christian Churches—not only a formal unity as expressed in Christ's will, but a concrete community.

According to Lukas Vischer,[19] this requires four conditions that must be fulfilled: (1) an explicit and unambiguous reconciliation between the individual Churches; (2) community in the

---

[16] Cf. "Crunch at the Council", in *Time* (Dec. 12, 1969), p. 37.

[17] Cf. A. Vanneste, "Théologie universelle et Théologie Africaine", in *Rev. du Clergé Africain*, 24 (May–July 1969), pp. 324–36; L. M. Colonnese, "The Church in Latin America: Imperialism or Servanthood?", in *The American Ecclesiastical Review*, CLXI (1969/2), pp. 100–13.

[18] See L. Vischer's report on this assembly, "Dialogue entre les Eglises: positif ou négatif?", in *IDOC* int. n. 11 (1969), pp. 2–13.

[19] *Ibid.*, pp. 5–9.

Eucharist; (3) the awareness of being united with the one Body of Christ, which implies the awareness of all belonging together, not only in the formal sense of being one with the Body of Christ but also in genuine responsibility for each other. And this means (4) that we look for suitable forms and structures and do not slip into centralization and meddlesomeness. This presupposes a much more thoroughgoing pluriformity; the Churches will have to prove that they can achieve real community, break down the walls that separate man from man, and bring families, classes, races and nationalities to a genuine unity.

Such a programme assumes a basic change in the existing ecclesiastical structures, which are considered to be unalterable—wrongly so, because in the course of history they have had constantly to adjust their structures, consciously or subconsciously, to those of society. The structures of tomorrow will also see the doctrinal differences of today in another light.

Vischer's idea often is too lightly brushed aside by Catholics with the uncompromising statement that they do not want any ecumenical experiments. An ecumenical movement is incompatible with that clinging to self-survival which besets so much ecclesiastical organization.

As one can gather from recent articles in various periodicals, developments are now beginning to take shape which point to another element in the new identity of the ecumenical movement: a true internationalization and universalization of the movement at the expense of its ecclesiasticism, but with the definite intention of preventing the necessary institutionalization of the Christian message in modern society from becoming sectarian.

The World Council is conscious that it has reached a turning-point in its lightning career. The Decree on Ecumenism of Vatican II, seen against the background of the preliminary discussions[20] and together with the Declaration on non-Christian Religions, shows the same broadening out towards the whole human world, and no longer limits the Church's service to the geographical boundaries of Christendom. Attention, however, has

---

[20] Cf. *Lex. f. Theol. u. Kirche, Vat. II*, vol. II (1967), "Einführung in das Dekret über den Ökumenismus", by W. Becker, pp. 11–39.

been drawn repeatedly to a certain discrepancy between the Decree on Ecumenism and that on the Eastern Churches.[21]

Those Churches that belong to the Lutheran World Federation are still mainly preoccupied with Church unity among themselves.[22] The most striking results seem to have been obtained in South India,[23] and the way in which all Protestant Churches now work together in France (*Conseil des Quatre Bureaux*) is truly exemplary.[24]

III. Dialogue with Islam

The effective blocking of the expansion of Christianity in the East by Islam in the fourteenth century is an historical fact which has for a long time prevented any effective dialogue between Christianity and Islam. The discovery of the new world by Spain had a liberating effect on Christianity in the fifteenth century: it created a new possibility of expansion. Now that hesitant attempts are made to set this dialogue going—Cardinal Marella speaks of timid steps forward[25]—Christianity is confronted with a liberalizing attempt at renewal within Islam which suffered a setback at the world assembly at Rabat,[26] and with the dogmatizing tendency of a more conservative-minded Mohammedanism[27] which wants to stress what the Christian faith and Islam have in common.

The first need here is a disposal of the prejudices that have been nourished by a centuries-old war mentality on both sides. Masson[28] has pointed to the positive value of the communal character of Islam, which is a community rather than a religion.

[21] M. Rinvolucri, *Anatomie d'une Eglise. L'Eglise Grecque d'aujourd'hui* (Paris, 1969), p. 169.

[22] M. Meyer, "Weltluthertum und Unionsproblem", in *Luth. Monatshefte*, 8 (1969/1), pp. 6–15.

[23] *Ibid.*, pp. 7–8.

[24] Cf. M. Lienhard, "Das lutherisch-reformierte Gespräch in Frankreich", in *Luth. Monatsh.*, 8 (1969/7), pp. 324–8.

[25] Quoted in *Inf. cath. intern.*, 347 (1 Nov. 1969), p. 22.

[26] Reported in *Inf. cath. intern.*, 346 (15 Oct. 1969), pp. 4–6. See also *IDOC* int. 13 (1969): "Chrétiens et pays arabes. Conclusions du congrès des étudiants chrétiens à Broumana (Liban). 10–16 juillet 1969", pp. 3–14.

[27] *Ibid.*

[28] "L'Islam: une religion et une communauté", in *Inf. cath. intern.*, 347 (1 Nov. 1969), pp. 23–5.

The Rabat Conference (22–25 September 1969) clearly showed the need for an internal ecumenical movement within Mohammedanism. This need was mainly prompted by the necessity of an economic link-up with the outside world. The suggestion made by the Lebanese President, Charles Hélou, to invite Christians to take part in this ecumenical movement was discreetly rejected by the Mohammedan authorities.[29]

The World Council, too, is bestirring itself to start an official dialogue between Christianity and Islam. Twenty-five representatives of both sides met from 2 to 9 March at Cartigny near Geneva in a conference which had been prepared by serious preliminary studies in 1968. The practical conclusions were limited to recognition of the need for such a dialogue.[30]

It is a great pity that this *rapprochement* was given an anti-Semitic twist when the results, minimal as they were, were immediately used to influence world opinion in favour of the Arab world and against Israel.[31] It has therefore been argued that a similar dialogue with Judaism must be set up if there are to be any real results.[32]

During his visit to Africa (August 1969) Pope Paul expressed his deep respect for Mohammedanism to the representatives of the Mohammedan community.[33] The official orientation of the Congregation for non-Christians has the same approach to the Christian–Mohammedan dialogue.[34]

It is important to realize that all these approaches stimulate ecumenical awareness, as P. Berger calls it.[35] Ecumenical awareness makes it possible to develop a theology that is perfectly aware of the full extent of man's religious pursuit in a way which is apparently wholly new in the history of religion. This will

---

[29] *Inf. cath. intern.*, 346 (15 Oct. 1969), p. 6.
[30] See "Conclusions du dialogue chrétiens-musulmans", in *IDOC* int. 5 (1969), pp. 3–6.
[31] Cf. M. P. Misk, "Dialogue Islamo-chrétien", in *Esprit*, 37 (1969/10), pp. 575–8.
[32] Cf. "Texte de la consultation sur le Moyen-Orient (Londres, mars 1969)", in *IDOC* int. 5 (1969), pp. 7–9, and J. B. Taylor, "Le dialogue entre chrétiens et musulmans", in *IDOC* int. 12 (1969), pp. 76–95.
[33] *Inf. cath. int.*, 347 (1 Oct. 1969), p. 22.
[34] "Orientation pour un dialogue entre chrétiens et musulmans", in publ. by Polyglotte vaticane, 1969, p. 160.
[35] Peter L. Berger, *A Rumor of Angels* (New York, 1969).

increase the probability that no authentic discovery of religious truth will be overlooked simply because the theologian happens to belong to another religion or another culture.

This last point also shows why ecumenical theology as a separate discipline is on the decline, because any theology, worthy of its name, has to be ecumenical today.[36]

IV. INTERRELIGIOUS ECUMENISM

This expression does not refer to a kind of syncretism such as we can observe it in the history of religion in times of religious decay. It implies the discovery of the richness of other religions. Today the theologian has at his disposal a vast treasure-house of information about religious thought during any historical period, and about all the existing religions, so that there is no longer the slightest excuse for theological ethnocentrism.

It is not as if Christians in the past were totally ignorant about the content of non-Christian religions. History relates that occasionally theological colloquies took place between representatives of different religions. In the thirteenth century, the Mongol Prince Mangu Khan organized such a colloquy. This experiment was repeated on a larger scale in the sixteenth century by the Emperor Akbar in India.

We should also mention here the powerful influence exercised by Max Müller's publication of the Sacred Books of the East in the last century,[37] and, at a more popular level, the excitement caused by the World Parliament of Religions, held in association with the World Exhibition of Chicago in 1893. The scientific achievements of those days are monumental and still basic to any study in the field of the history of religions, even though they are occasionally dubbed "premature ecumenism".

This confrontation of Christianity with other religions has

---

[36] Cf. J. Brosseder, "Ecumenical Theology", in *Sacramentum Mundi*, II (1968), pp. 204 ff. (with bibl.).

[37] Cf. C. B. Papali, "Exkurs zum Konzilstext über den Hinduismus", and H. Dumoulin, "Exkurs zum Konzilstext über den Buddhismus", in *Lex. f. Theol. u. Kirche*, Suppl. II (1967), pp. 478–82 and 482–5 (with bibl.); see also "The role of sacred writings in different religious communities", in *Concilium* (Documentation), 10, 3 (Dec. 1967), pp. 70–83 (American edn., vol. 30, pp. 143–73).

been intensified by political developments, the growing self-awareness of young Churches in developing countries, and missionary contacts with the true spirit of other religions. The result has been the present recognition of the genuine revelatory character of these non-Christian religions; revelation is no longer seen as coinciding with christology.

Buddhist and Hindu spirituality, in particular, show an affinity with what Christian spirituality has acknowledged as authentic religious experience.[38] The days of an expansion of Christianity on the lines of spiritual colonialism are gone, and in periodicals like *The Buddhist* there are vehement protests against the building of Christian churches in regions that are wholly Buddhist.[39]

Panikkar even talks about the unknown Christ in Hinduism, and the need for the Christian to recognize God's self-communication also in these great living religions which impressed their religious orientation on the majority of mankind, and still do so.[40]

The question is now how to formulate Christianity anew in a non-European culture and in non-European terms.[41] Panikkar also points out that this confrontation of Christianity with Buddhism will help Buddhists and Hindus to see Christianity as less of a sect and as more of a universal religion.

The dialogue between different religions was initiated by the Buddhists.[42] In 1955 J. Ulliana was invited by a Buddhist College to become Professor of Catholicism, a post specially set up for

[38] Cf. A. Ravier (ed.), *La Mystique et les mystiques* (1965); G. Siegmund, "Longing for God as a General Basis for Dialogue", in *Concilium*, 9, 3 (Nov. 1967), pp. 63–9 (American edn., vol. 29, pp. 137–53); H. Dumoulin, "A Meeting with Zen-Buddhists", in *Concilium* 9, 3 (Nov. 1967), pp. 70–7 (American edn., vol. 29, pp. 155–74); A. de Groot, "The Missions after Vatican II", in *Concilium*, 6, 4 (June 1968), pp. 82–90 (American edn., vol. 36, pp. 160–80); Thomas Merton was interested in this question throughout his life, cf. "In Memory of Thomas Merton", in *Continuum*, 7 (1969, 2).

[39] *The Buddhist*, XL, Poson 2513 (June 1969, 2), reprinted in *Quest*, IV (1969, 35 and 36) pp. 166 f. *The Buddhist* is the magazine of the "Colombo Young Men's Buddhist Association".

[40] R. Panikkar, *Le Christ inconnu de l'Hindouisme* (1964).

[41] *Id.*, "Confrontation between Hinduism and Christ", in *Logos*, 10 (1969, 2), pp. 43–51.

[42] J. Ulliana, "Christianity and Buddhism in Thailand", in *Logos*, 10

this purpose. This meant that Thai Catholics could emerge from their self-made ghetto. Today Thailand has a Department of Religion which each year organizes a study week to bring various religions together in order to discuss a previously fixed theme, such as "Religion brings peace" or "A man is good if he has a religion", and so on.[43] At such meetings Christianity is treated on an equal footing with Buddhism and Islam.

Ceylon, too, has its Congress of Religions, where all the main religions of the country (Buddhism, Hinduism and Christianity) are represented.[44] This Congress also organizes annual conferences where themes of a general nature, such as "Good Citizenship", are discussed by the representatives of each religion. It seems that this has had a remarkable influence on the relations between the various religions. Similar institutions also exist in Vietnam and Indonesia, but are dominated by the State.[45]

It should be clear that these ecumenical movements are not meant to reduce the other religions to Christianity, or vice versa. The basic religious experiences of other religions and the religious attitude that springs from them are taken seriously, broaden the ecumenical awareness of all, and offer theology new opportunities of integrating the experiential aspect of religion into the whole theological argument.

Although all this does not yet show results in any concrete form, it is easy to see that this kind of confrontation makes for a fruitful and inspiring theology, also in those young Christian Churches. And this is another feature which helps the ecumenical movement to discover its identity more clearly.

V. The Dialogue with Marxism

If ecumenism is readily understood as implying religion when it operates among Christians of various denominations or between Christianity and other religions, this is not the case when it is applied to a dialogue between Christians and Marxists.[46] Some

---

(1969, 2), pp. 52–6, reprinted from the *Bulletin* of the Secretariat for non-Christians, 11 (June 1969).   [43] *Ibid.*

[44] Cf. T. Balasuriya, "Christian-Buddhist Dialogue in Ceylon", in *Logos,* 10 (1969, 1), pp. 33–9.   [45] *Ibid.*, pp. 38 f.

[46] For the problem of the dialogue, cf. Dubarle, "Der Dialog und die

will wonder between what kind of Christians and what kind of Marxists this dialogue is supposed to take place. The very question already implies a certain mistrust of those Christians and Marxists who feel inclined to take part in such a dialogue. The complicated situation which has recently arisen with regard to such figures as Garaudy[47] and Girardi[48] shows that this mistrust is not limited to a mere implication.

The reports on the study days organized by the *Paulusgesellschaft*, or those on the conference organized by the World Council in Geneva in April 1968,[49] or the well-informed articles on the Christian-Marxist dialogue that have appeared in the international review *Dialog*,[50] all show that this dialogue is not a superficial phenomenon.

For Christians living under a Marxist regime it has been a healthy experience to face up to honest questions put by Marxists, and it has certainly opened up new perspectives for the theologians, in Poland, for instance. From being a "silent" Church they have again begun to speak.[51] Such a dialogue does not only help the Churches but also Marxism itself, since both may cease to inspire once they become too dogmatic and too institutionalized.[52] On a study day organized by the British Council of

Philosophie des Dialogs", in *Int. Dialog. Zeitschr.*, 1 (1968), pp. 3–14; P. Blanquart, "Die Diskussion über den Humanismus bei den französischen Kommunisten und ihre Auswirkungen auf den Dialog mit den Christen", in *Int. Dialog Zeitschr.*, 1 (1968, 1), pp. 118–27.

[47] R. Garaudy, *Le grand tournant du socialisme* (Paris, 1969).

[48] Cf. the dialogue between G. Girardi and Y. Congar in *Inf. cath. intern.*, 351 (1 Jan. 1970), pp. 29 f., which, as a whole, is informative for the present situation (pp. 21–36).

[49] Cf. W. Hollitscher, "Religion und Revolution. Bericht über eine Dialogtagung", in *Int. Dialog Zeitschr.*, 2 (1969, 1), pp. 91–4.

[50] P. Hebblethwaite, "Dialog in England", in *Int. Dialog Zeitschr.*, 1 (1968, 1), pp. 99 f.; E. Kadlecová, "Die Gespräche in Marienbad", *ibid.*, pp. 101–9; M. Machovec, "Dialog in der Tschechoslowakei", *ibid.* (1968, 3), pp. 298–316; C. Perrotta, "Der Dialog in Italien", *ibid.*, 2 (1969, 3), pp. 278–87; V. Gardavsky, "Der Dialog in Amerika", *ibid.*, 2 (1969, 2), pp. 187 f.

[51] "Après la première phase du dialogue entre chrétiens et marxistes", in *Vigilia*, 33, 2 (Feb. 1968), pp. 141–3; W. D. Marsch, "Bedingungen und Grenzen einer Verständigung zwischen Christen und Marxisten", in *Zeitschr. f. Evang. Ethik*, 12, 1 (Jan. 1968), pp. 36–44; "Christians and Communists in Search of Man", in *Theology*, 70,570 (Dec. 1967), the whole number.

[52] J. Ladrière, *Anthropologie du Marxisme* (Paris, n.d.); Louis Althusser,

Churches in 1967, a Marxist remarked that the debate about God was not reserved to Christians but also affected Marxists.[53]

Apart from an inward ecumenical movement, there is also room for an outward-going one. The confrontation between all religious convictions should lead to a situation where belief is no longer divisive but unifying, and thus can play its part in the unification of mankind. The basis of the ecumenical dialogue remains the historical solidarity of mankind, in the vital awareness that this solidarity is constantly threatened, and that we are therefore constantly challenged by the need to build it up actively and effectively.

There is no room here for a detailed treatment of the very complex ecumenical relations between Judaism and Christianity.[54] It would not, however, have made any difference to the general thesis that during the last fifty years the ecumenical movement has been feeling its way towards a deeper identity and a deeper self-awareness. The movement must stimulate all religions to become aware of their essentially unifying function for the effective unification of the whole inhabited world.[55]

Pour Marx (Coll. Théorie, ed. Maspéro, 1967); T. Pluzanski, " 'Dialogue' avec le marxisme dans la conception de Jean Yves Calvez", in *Argumentow*, 4, 33 (1967), pp. 122–9.

[53] *Inf. cath. intern.*, 299 (1 Nov. 1967), p. 22.

[54] Since 1965 the Service de documentation judéo-chrétienne (SIDIC) has been publishing a very good bulletin which can be obtained gratis by anyone interested.

[55] I. Anastasiou, *The use of the word "ecumenical" in connection with the Ecumenical Councils* (Salonica, 1966); cf. the multilingual *Oecumenica* —Annales de recherches théologiques (Paris, Geneva, Minneapolis, Gütersloch, 1969). In recent years the word "dialogue" has acquired many connotations; the terms "inter-humanistic dialogue", "inter-religious dialogue", "inter-covenantal dialogue" (between the two covenants) and "inter-confessional dialogue" are used with a specific meaning: cf. J. Aagaard, "Witness and Dialogue in a Missionary Perspective", in *Oecumenica*, and A. van der Bent "Le Conseil oecuménique des Eglises face au défi d'un dialogue oecuménique", in *IDOC*, 14 (15 Dec. 1969), pp. 73–91.

Translated by Theo Westow

PAPA'S LEMONADE

GREENWILLOW BOOKS

EVE RICE

PAPA'S LEMONADE

AND OTHER STORIES

A DIVISION OF WILLIAM MORROW & COMPANY, INC. | NEW YORK

For HHR,
with all my love

Library of Congress Cataloging in Publication Data
Rice, Eve.   Papa's lemonade and other stories.
(Greenwillow read-alone)   Contents: Pennies. — A garden.
— A nice walk. — Missing. — Papa's lemonade. [1. Family life — Fiction.
2. Short stories]   I. Title.   PZ7.R3622Pap   [E]   75-38754
ISBN 0-688-80041-6   ISBN 0-688-84041-8 lib. bdg.

CONTENTS

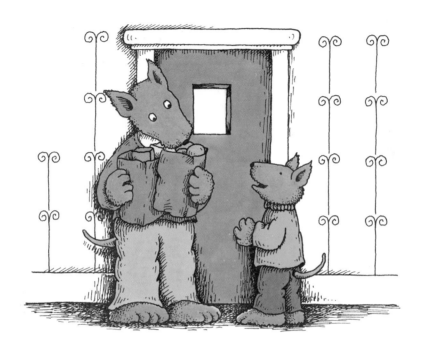

PENNIES

Papa walked into the kitchen.

He had been shopping.

"Papa, Papa! Do you have

any pennies?" asked Freddie.

"Pennies?" said Molly.

"Pennies?" said Sam.

"Does Papa have pennies?"
asked Nora.

And a little voice said,

"Oh, goodie! Pennies!" It was Jasper.

"Now, now," said Mama. "At least

let Papa put his things down."

Papa put the bags on the table.

He looked in his pockets for pennies.

"Here," he said.

Papa had a handful of pennies.

He gave each of the children two.

Freddie put his pennies

in his bank—"clink, clink."

Molly dropped hers in.

"Clink, clink."

And Sam. And Nora.

Jasper dropped his pennies in his bank.

And then something awful happened.

Jasper dropped his bank.

And there he stood,

in the middle of all his pennies.

Jasper sniffled.

"Don't cry," said Papa.

"Don't cry," said Mama.

"We will find you a new bank.

Let me see."

Mama took a big bottle

down from the shelf.

"Does this look like a bank

for Jasper?"

"No," said Sam.

"Uh, uh," said Molly.

And Jasper sniffled again.

So Mama put it back.

She took down
a square tin.
"Is this a bank?"
"No," said Freddie.
"It's a cooky tin."

"How about this?"
asked Mama.
"It's a sugar bowl,"
said Nora.
Jasper frowned.

Mama thought hard.
"There must be
a bank for Jasper
somewhere."

She moved the ketchup and the sugar.

"Here it is!" she said.

Mama had an empty honey jar

shaped like a little bear.

"A bear bank for Jasper?"

Jasper smiled. "A bear bank!"

"A bear bank is a fine bank," said Papa,

"and every bit as good as a piggy bank."

Mama gave the bear bank to Jasper.

Then Mama and Papa,

Molly, Freddie, Nora, Sam, and Jasper

picked up all the pennies.

They put them in Jasper's new bank.

"There," said Mama.

"There," said Jasper.

"There," said Papa. "And what
  a nice family of banks we have—
  four little pigs and one fine bear."

A GARDEN

When they had picked up the bits
of Jasper's old bank, Mama said,
"It's too nice a day to stay inside.
Why don't you go out and play?"
"It's too hot," said Freddie.
"I don't want to," Molly said.

"Me neither," said Sam.

"Uh, uh," said Nora.

Jasper didn't say a word.

"All right," Papa said.

"Mama and I are going outside."

"Good-bye!" called Mama and Papa

as they walked out the door.

"Good-bye," called the children.

Mama and Papa
stood in the sunshine.
"Wouldn't it be nice to have
a garden?" Mama asked.
"Yes, indeed," said Papa.
"We could plant a garden
by the cherry tree.
I will get a shovel."

"Wait," said Mama. "We have nothing
    to put in our garden yet."

"True," Papa said.

"But we can dig out the rocks.
    Good gardens don't have rocks."

"First, let's think
    what we will plant.
    Then we can dig," said Mama.

They sat down under the cherry tree
and closed their eyes to think better.

"Strawberries," said Mama after a minute.

"Mmmmmm. Strawberries," said Papa.

"That will be nice.

We can have strawberries

like the ones that grow in the woods."

"Yes," Mama said. "And what else?"

"Grapes," said Papa.

"For jam," Mama said. "Jam grapes

like the ones that grow by the lake."

"And what else?" asked Papa.

"Onions—the kind that grow

along the road.

Then we can make onion soup."

"I love onion soup," Papa said,

"and carrots too."

"Mmmmmm. Like the wild carrots

from the field," said Mama.

She thought some more.

"You know?" she said.

"What?" asked Papa.

"We don't really need a garden at all.
   What we need is a nice walk
   along the road, across the field,
   and down to the lake."

"Good idea," said Papa.

"And then I don't need a shovel.

But I do need my walking stick."

"And I will take my basket,"

Mama said, "to fill with good things

along the way."

A NICE WALK

It took Papa a little while
to find his walking stick.
Then they were ready.

Mama and Papa
walked down the road.
Mama swung her basket.

They walked past a little house.

"Hello! Nice day!" called a skunk.

"Hello to you," said Mama and Papa.

"We are off on a walk

down to the lake."

"Have a nice walk," said the skunk.

"Have a nice day," said Mama and Papa.

And off they went across the field.

A rabbit came hopping.

"Well, hello there," said Mama.

"Hello, hello," the rabbit said.

"Lovely grass for nibbling here."

"We're going down to the lake,"
  said Papa.

"Have a nice time," said the rabbit.

"And good day to you," Mama said.

They walked on into the woods.

They passed an old tree.

Two squirrels poked their heads out.

"Hello!"

"Hello!"

"What a fine tree," said Mama.

"Stop and have some tea?"

"We're on our way down to the lake,"
Papa said.

"Well, have a nice walk then,"
the squirrel said.

"Thank you!" called Mama and Papa
over their shoulders. "Good-bye!"

Mama and Papa came to the lake.

They dipped their paws in the water

and made ripples.

Then they walked home.

"Oh, I'm tired," said Mama.

"I am too," said Papa

and sat on the front step.

Mama put her basket down.

"Oh, Papa! I was so busy

saying hello that I forgot

all about the carrots!"

"And I forgot too," said Papa.

"No strawberries either," said Mama.

"No grapes. No onions.

Now we cannot make onion soup."

"No onion soup," said Papa.
"But we had a nice walk
and we have nice friends.
And that's even better than
onion soup."

MISSING

When Papa had rested a minute,

he felt better.

Mama got up and opened the door.

"Something is strange," she said.

"What?" asked Papa.

"I am quite sure it is too quiet

for a house with five children."

Papa listened.

It was very quiet.

"Yes," said Papa.

"I think there are no children

in this house at all."

"No children—but lots of paw prints,"

said Mama.

"Aha!" Papa said.

"Let's see where they go."

Mama and Papa

followed the tracks.

The paw prints stopped

at the back door.

Papa opened the door.

"There they are. They are sitting
on the rock," said Mama.

"But I do not think they are all there."

She counted heads.

"One, two, three, four . . . four.

We are missing a child."

"Missing?" said Papa. "Let me count.

One, two, three, four.

Yes," Papa said.

"We are missing a child."

"Now," said Mama. "Who is missing?"

"Who is missing?" said Papa.

"Who is missing?" said a little voice.

Mama and Papa turned around.

There was Jasper.

"That is the child
who is missing," said Mama.

"The missing child," Papa said.

"I am not missing," said Jasper.

"I am right here."

"You are indeed," said Papa.

"So now we can stop looking.

And since I don't have to look

for you, I can make some lemonade."

"Lemonade?" said Jasper. "Mmmm."

"Fine," Mama said.

"We can all have lemonade."

"Children!" called Mama.

Not an ear twitched.

"Lemonade!" Mama called.

And all the ears turned.

"Wow! Lemonade!"

And they all came running.

PAPA'S LEMONADE

Everyone went into the kitchen.

"Now for the lemonade," said Papa.

He went to get the lemons.

"No lemons?" asked Papa.

"There are oranges,

but I do not see any lemons.

Where have they all gone?"

"Jasper ate them" said Molly.

"That's silly," said Mama.

Mama looked at Jasper.

Jasper looked a little sour.

"Jasper, did you eat the lemons?"

Jasper would not look at Mama

or Papa so they all knew

that he had eaten the lemons.

"Oh, Jasper!" said Mama.

"That is very hard to believe."

"Yes," said Papa.

"And it is very hard to make

lemonade without any lemons.

But I will try."

Papa got the oranges.

He squeezed them into a jug.

Then he added water

and sugar and stirred it all.

"Now," he said, "lemonade!"

"Orangeade," whispered Nora.

"I heard that," Papa said.
He filled the glasses
and sat down.

"Now," Papa said, "we will all
think very lemon thoughts."
"Sour," said Sam.
They all took a sip.
"It tastes like orange juice,"
said Freddie.

"You are not thinking hard enough,"
  Papa said.

"Think more lemon thoughts."

"Yellow," Molly said.

"Very, very sour," said Nora.

"Shiny, bumpy outside," said Freddie.

"Doesn't roll right," said Jasper.

  Molly looked at Jasper.

"Well, it doesn't," Jasper said.

"It isn't round."

"Lemony lemonade," said Mama.

"Lemony lemonade," they all said

and took another sip.

"Maybe it does taste a little
like lemonade," Nora said.
"A little? It tastes a lot
like lemonade!" said Papa.

Mama laughed.

"It is the best lemonade made with oranges that I have ever had."

They all laughed.

And they all took another sip . . .

and another . . .

and another . . .

and finished Papa's lemonade

right down to the very last drop.